Music Advocacy

Moving from Survival to Vision

John L. Benham

Published in partnership with
MENC: The National Association for Music Education

ROWMAN & LITTLEFIELD EDUCATION
A division of
ROWMAN & LITTLEFIELD PUBLISHERS, INC.
Lanham • New York • Toronto • Plymouth, UK

Published in partnership with MENC: The National Association for Music Education

Published by Rowman & Littlefield Education
A division of Rowman & Littlefield Publishers, Inc.
A wholly owned subsidary of The Rowman & Littlefield Publishing Group, Inc.
4501 Forbes Boulevard, Suite 200, Lanham, Maryland 20706
http://www.rowmaneducation.com

Estover Road, Plymouth PL6 7PY, United Kingdom

British Library Cataloguing in Publication Information Available

Library of Congress Cataloging-in-Publication Data

Benham, John L., 1942–
  Music advocacy : moving from survival to vision / John L. Benham.
      p. cm.
  "Published in partnership with MENC: The National Association for Music Education."
  Includes bibliographical references and index.
  ISBN 978-1-60709-780-8 (cloth : alk. paper)—ISBN 978-1-60709-781-5 (pbk. : alk. paper)—ISBN 978-1-60709-782-2 (electronic)
  1. School music—Instruction and study—United States. 2. School management and organization—United States. I. Title.
  MT1.B523 2011
  780.71—dc22

                                                                    2010029690

∞ ™ The paper used in this publication meets the minimum requirements of American National Standard for Information Sciences—Permanence of Paper for Printed Library Materials, ANSI/NISO Z39.48-1992.

Printed in the United States of America

This book is dedicated to . . .

Jessica, Maegan, Lauren, Erik, Benjamin, Cody, Carter, Caysa, Cora
. . . and the thousands of other students who will continue to
make music as we allow and equip them.

Contents

Figures

Tables

How to Use This Book

This is not a book about the philosophy of music education. Many other texts exist that can provide you with that information. Rather, this is a resource that assumes you agree with the author that *access to a quality music education is the right of every student and the responsibility of every school district and community.*

The materials in this text are designed to provide you with data related to preserving music programs that may be threatened by budget reductions, efforts at educational reform, or other factors that may prevent or reduce opportunities for students to make music. This same information may be used as a means of expanding current music programs or developing new ones. This information may not only help you save or build your program, but also is essential to understanding how to function in an educational system that so often can appear to be dysfunctional.

The information contained in this text has been assembled from data collected by the author since 1981, the year in which he first developed the concept of *reverse economics*. The data represents consulting efforts with over 300 school districts in nearly every state and province in North America. (*Note:* Most of the data used in the various subjects discussed in this text are based on data collected from instrumental music programs. Unfortunately, there is little similar data related to choral programs. However, the information and principles remain the same for choral programs and general music.)

This is not fiction or theory. The methods presented in this text have been successfully applied in saving over $70 million of proposed budgetary reductions in music programs. The results represent the saving of over 2,000 music teacher positions and the annual opportunity for over 500,000 students to continue making music.

In the words of one public school administrator, gaining access to this information is like taking a graduate course in music administration. This material is essential for music administrators, department chairs, and individual music teachers in those districts without music administrators.

There are several major players in negotiating for the establishment, expansion, or saving of music programs. These subject areas form the primary sections of this text. The final section is a collection of practical suggestions and appendices of materials related to successful music advocacy. The more familiar you are with these materials the more apt you are to be successful in your endeavors to provide opportunities for all students to make music.

The Music Coalition: Chapter 2 describes necessary components of a well-organized local music coalition. It elevates the typical music "booster" organization beyond the typical fundraiser model to one that provides the political structure and power for ensuring a positive environment for maintaining and building music programs for students.

The School System: The information presented in chapter 3 provides you with a clearer understanding of how the system functions in the decision-making process. It defines the unique roles of the various decision makers, including the school board and the administration.

The Profession: In chapter 4, the role of the music educator in advocacy is presented from the perspective of a unified philosophy and curriculum. Professional unity is a primary key to successful music advocacy.

The Process: While the keys to successful advocacy are primarily political, the collection and presentation of appropriate data is often the key to winning the final decision. Beginning with chapter 5, the process of advocacy is presented from the initial collection and interpretation of data to the development and presentation of the proposal, and suggestions for following up decisions to ensure their implementation.

A collection of information on various topics related to the text is included in a series of appendixes. Basic to understanding these materials is acquisition of a vocabulary that enables the music educator to speak "educese." A glossary of terms is provided in the appendixes to assist you in the development of your communication skills within the education system.

Acknowledgments

Music education has a great heritage of advocates who first established the concept of music education in the schools. We not only owe these people a great debt for their efforts, but we also have the obligation to continue their efforts. We do this through our continual striving for excellence in teaching and learning; and we do it through our efforts as advocates of music for all children.

The glamour of hotels, restaurants, and airports that comes with a heavy travel schedule wears off very quickly. However, the lives of spouses and children who are left at home are no less affected. I cannot begin to adequately express appreciation for the understanding support of my wife Merridee and our children Stephen, Melody, and Todd.

I am thankful for the experience of six years on the school board of the Moundsview School District 621 (Minnesota). I have often stated that I learned more in those years about the educational system than in all my years of education and teaching. The music teachers in that district not only provided my children with an excellent music experience, but also modeled exemplary unity as educators.

The music industry has been the leader in music advocacy and the support of my efforts as a consultant. They have provided the motivation and means for music educators to become advocates. While some may say that those efforts were self-serving, it is my observation that there are few people who care more about their customers than these people. Of note are Kurt Karls (Schmitt Music Company), who first made the industry aware of my advocacy efforts, Karl Bruhn (NAMM), who served as a primary mentor in developing my materials, and Mike Bennett (National Association of Band Instrument Manufacturers—we first met as college students in band and working at B.A. Rose Music), who envisioned the "superfund" that provided much of the funding for my consultant efforts.

NAMM (National Association of Music Merchants) has assumed leadership in the cause as advocates for music education. The organization is the leader in funding research on music and the brain, the development of the concept of a national music coalition, and the establishment of government relations for the advancement of music education. In many ways it is their establishment of Support Music (see *Counterpoint* and the *SupportMusic Community Action Kit* at www.supportmusic.com) that continues to lead the advocacy movement. A special word of appreciation is due Mary Luehrsen and Sandra Jordan.

I would like to express my appreciation to Debra Bresnan for her editing skills. She has a unique ability to convert the technical language of "educese" into the vernacular. Many of the materials contained in this book have been processed by her translation skills.

Finally, some of the entries contained in these chapters are contributions of my son, Stephen Benham (Ph.D., Eastman School of Music). These are acknowledged within the body of the text.

I

THE BASICS OF
MUSIC ADVOCACY

1

Music Cuts: Politics, Budgets, and Reform

Music education exists because of those initial advocates who first saw to it that students were provided with the opportunities to learn and make music. Music education continues because of a multitude of people and organizations that have come to recognize the importance of making music for the intellectual, emotional, and social development of children in our schools. The Association for Supervision and Curriculum Development (ASCD) affirmed the importance of music education in 1989, when its 126,000 members adopted the following resolution supporting the inclusion of the visual and performing arts in a balanced curriculum.

> With recent focus on specific subject matter, academic achievement, and a series of reform efforts/movements that emphasize raising test scores and graduation requirements, a balance of curriculum offerings is not being maintained. Dance, drama, music, and the *visual and performing arts are disciplines with aesthetic, perceptual, creative, and intellectual dimensions.* They foster students' abilities to create, experience, analyze, and reorganize, thereby *encouraging intuitive and emotional responses.* The arts can increase self-discipline and motivation, contribute to a positive self-image, provide an acceptable outlet for emotions, and help to *develop creative and intuitive thinking processes not always inherent in other academic disciplines.*
>
> ASCD supports the concept that *arts education is essential in a balanced curriculum* and urges educators to include the visual and performing arts at all appropriate levels of education. The Association encourages educators to explore opportunities to integrate the arts in an interdisciplinary approach to education and seek a variety of techniques to assess such an approach. (ASCD Board of Directors Minutes, March 1989; emphasis added)

Reinforcing its position of the importance of arts education for every child, the ASCD subsequently published a book on the subject by Eric Jensen. In *Arts with the Brain in Mind*, the ASCD provides credibility to the publication on the copyright page by clearly stating that "there was no financial support or any other potential conflict of interest from any of the many fine organizations that commonly support the arts" (Jensen, 2000, preface). In stating his biases the author indicates that he is in no traditional sense an artist, but above all an "advocate for improving education."

The thesis of the book is that "arts are not only fundamental to success in our demanding, highly technical, fast-moving world, but they are what makes us most human, most complete as people." Further, from all the research the "facts are in: You can make as good a case, or better, for arts than you can make for any other discipline." Jensen states, "The fact is, humans are unique; and educators need different approaches and strategies to reach a wide range of learners. Believe it or not, many schools, districts, and states have been using a powerful solution for decades. It's called the arts."

In the last half of the twentieth century events such as the Russian launching of Sputnik, the publication of *Nation at Risk*, and the passing of Proposition 13 in California stimulated a voracious appetite for cutting music programs. As a resident of the state of California from 1975 to 1981, I witnessed the destruction of one public school music program after another. Unfortunately, the trend continues even today, as many public school leaders are products of districts in which they had no opportunity to participate in music, and therefore have no experiential understanding of its role in education.

In 1981, my family and I moved to Minnesota. We were careful to establish residency in a school district with outstanding academic and music programs. It would provide our children with a music curriculum spanning all grades and opportunities to make music in band, orchestra, and choir.

The week after we moved into the district, voters denied an $8,000,000 levy referendum that would have provided money needed to maintain all current programs. When the levy failed the district mandated a 70 percent reduction in orchestra staff and a 48 percent reduction in band staff. We were never able to determine the plans for reducing the general music or choral programs.

As a music educator (not teaching in the district) and member of the community, I joined with the local music coalition to fight any reductions in the music program. Initially we determined that we would present the most powerful philosophical case for saving the program that had ever been developed. On further analysis, we recognized that all seven board members and the superintendent had children in the instrumental music programs. They did not want to cut music, but assumed they had no other choice. It was obvious: we had to come up with other supporting reasons, preferably economic.

I requested basic information on the school district and data related to the number of students participating in the various programs. There was the answer! The number of students participating in the program was huge, to the extent that the average music teacher had sixty to seventy more students in the total class load than the regular classroom teacher. This gave the music teacher a full-time equivalent (FTE) value 60 percent greater than other teachers. The concept of *reverse economics* was born. The data clearly demonstrated that the district would lose more money by cutting the program than the initial savings it anticipated. The findings of the research were presented to the school board before an audience of several hundred parents. The school board reversed their decision, and the district reinstated all music positions. The district subsequently eliminated 150 teaching positions (approximately one out of every five teachers), and not one of them was in music.

News of the success of the parent effort and the process implemented in our district spread rapidly across the state and subsequently the nation. Other districts in Minnesota began to request assistance. The Minnesota Music Educators Association, the music industry (music retailers), the National Association of Band Instrument Manufacturers, the National Association of School Music Dealers, NAMM (the National Association of Music Merchants), and eventually the Music Educators National Conference heard about the Minnesota results.

Once NAMM and the National Association of Band Instrument Manufacturers (NABIM) became involved in advocacy, efforts became more nationalized, organized, and strategic. As MENC and its various affiliates joined the endeavor, the National Coalition for Music Education was formed. Membership in the movement has grown to massive proportions as numerous organizations have joined in the endeavor.

Advocating for music education? Just having to think and worry about defending something so valuable to every child can make us feel helpless and indignant in the same breath. But if you're a parent of a young person who enjoys making music, you may have already experienced firsthand the necessity of becoming involved; and if you're a community member who loves music, you know how much music education has enriched your life.

The truth is, we have no choice but to defend school music programs. In a time of drastic reductions in school budgets, music is often incorrectly perceived as non-core in the academic curriculum. As an advocate of music education, you already know that participation in music is vital to a young person's academic and social development: now it's up to you to make sure that music education programs in your community continue and flourish.

There is much to do. As of the most recent reports from MENC, only about 50 percent of the schools in the United States offer a quality music education for their students, and the American String Teacher's Association (ASTA) reports that only about 20 percent of the schools offer strings. It is the primary purpose of this text to assist you in advocating for music education in your school district.

WHAT IS A CUT, AND HOW DO YOU FIND THEM?

Music cuts are any factors or actions that negatively impact a student's potential to learn through participation in music programs. Threats to music programs normally come in one of two forms:

1. Budgetary issues: Enrollment decline, funding deficiencies, preference for funding other areas such as the perceived "basics" (i.e., math, English, science)
2. Educational reform: Middle schools or junior highs, scheduling, school-to-work, tax vouchers, charter or magnet schools

Fortunately for us, music advocacy has been with us since public school music education began. You can draw on the valuable experience of advocates who have been successful before you and still make new strides on behalf of music education in our current educational climate.

As a music advocate, you have a choice: you can wait until you hear of decisions that cut into young people's access to music making in your community, and then jump into the fray; or you can become better at recognizing the threat before it happens and keep your school's music programs off the list of cuts. I hope you'll do the latter.

Some music program budget cuts are easy to spot because the word *music* is in the line item of the budget or other documents published by the district. It is more difficult—yet certainly not impossible—to identify potential "hidden cuts" or budget line items that do not include the word *music*. This book will show you how to identify, and respond to, both potential and hidden cuts. Remember Rule #1!

Rule #1: No cut or compromise should be suggested by any member of the community. This includes the music coalition, music educators, and the music supervisor.

* * * * *

Suggest a cut or compromise, and you become responsible for the decision!

THE ADMINISTRATION MUST BALANCE THE BUDGET

I have never met an educator who became a school administrator because he or she wanted to eliminate music or any other program. However, it is a part of the administrative responsibility to balance the district budget. Administrators have varying degrees of decision-making powers and responsibilities related to the budget. Decisions that affect the quality of the music program are made at both the district level (school board, central administration, superintendent) and at each local school site (principal). Administrative powers and responsibilities will be covered in greater detail in chapter 3, "The School System."

In the process of recommending budget reductions or cuts, several events may occur:

- The district school board adopts a set of budget assumptions as recommended by the administration. These assumptions are used as a guide during the decision-making process.
- Central and site administrators present to the board a consensus philosophy and a list of priorities about which programs are essential and which programs should be cut.
- Community surveys are taken to give the administration a sense of what cuts may be most politically acceptable. These surveys may or may not be scientific and are often completely ignored during the decision-making process. They may only serve to give an illusion of community involvement.
- Music teachers are contacted individually or as a group (such as band teachers) and asked which reductions will do the least damage to the program. Any suggestion made will most certainly be accepted and cuts will be blamed on the teachers. If teachers from one area or music curriculum level suggest cuts in another area, this divides the music staff and converts music educators into music competitors. Keep in mind the old adage "united we stand, divided we fall" and repeat after me: "Any cuts will have a negative impact on student participation in music."

As you investigate the potential for cuts in your district, review all documents related to the budgetary decision-making process. This information is public and by law should be made available to members of your music coalition.

Any budget line item that includes the word *music* is a potential target when the district develops its list of cuts being proposed or considered. The proposed cuts publicized by the (central) administration to the school board normally identify only those specific music cuts that are a part of the central budget. Usually this includes cuts to elementary (general/vocal and instrumental) music programs that are staffed by itinerant teachers.

UNCOVERING THE HIDDEN CUTS

Hidden cuts include potential reductions to the music program that do not specifically identify music. Cuts at the secondary level most often fall into this category.

In analyzing the potential for hidden cuts in your district, be on the lookout for the following key words or phrases:

Across the board
After school
Alternative schools
Average
Charter schools
Clerical
Capital outlay
Cocurricular
Coordinators
Curricular
Department chairs
District-wide
Enrollment decline
Equal cuts
Extracurricular
Educational reform
Graduation requirements
Increase class size
Increase test scores
Magnet schools
Materials and supplies
Participation fees
Pay-to-play
Pull-outs
Reduce elective options
Reduce length of day
Reduce periods
Reduce staffing
School-to-work
Supervisors
Summer school
Surveys
Transportation

If these words or phrases appear in administrative proposals for budget cuts, odds are good that music cuts are being considered. You should immediately examine each proposal (before it is adopted by the board), paying particular attention to each line item in the district budget to see if it may contain items related to music.

You may or may not be informed of the specific details of hidden cuts. In my experience, the normal practice is to keep them as quiet as possible to avoid public confrontation. It is also typical to inform the music teachers but order them to not make proposed cuts public or face losing their jobs.

The latter course of action is, of course, illegal; but it does put the "fear" in teachers. Music teachers often fail to advocate against proposed cuts for this specific reason. To me, it seems completely illogical. If the district is eliminating teaching positions in music and music teachers don't fight it, they lose either way—and so do the students. And because low-seniority teachers are cut first, senior teachers may sometimes resist advocacy efforts to preserve their own jobs while sacrificing opportunities for children to participate in music.

CONVEYING THE NEGATIVE IMPACT OF MUSIC PROGRAM CUTS

Your school board may not even be aware of the potential impact of the hidden cuts on the music program. But remember: *a cut is any decision made that will negatively impact the ability of any student to participate in making music.*

Here are a few suggestions to assist you in avoiding cuts to your music programs:

- You would be wise to maintain open and continuous communication with your central and site administrators. This is a great role for the music coalition. When you keep the lines open, you lay a solid foundation for effective communication and problem solving in times of change or crisis.
- Keep in mind that any decisions that affect the ability to deliver a quality music program are made not only at the district (board and central administration) level, but also at each local school site.
- Beware of proposals to make equal cuts "across the board" because music programs normally have more line items than other curricular areas. This means that across the board cuts can be particularly damaging to music programs.
- The proper role for the music advocate is defender of the music program. Well-researched and clearly presented impact statements are key to a successful defense. Impact statements are basically response arguments and statements such as this: "If the administration adopts the proposed recommendation for cuts in the music program, it will have the following short- and long-term impacts on the faculty, curriculum, student participation, and the budget."

- And finally, always remember: *no member of the music staff or community should suggest cuts or compromises!* Doing so transfers the responsibility for making cuts from the administration to the music teacher, music supervisor, or music coalition.

> Effective Advocacy = Accurate Information + Clear Communication
> + Long-Range Strategies

As committed music advocates and thoughtful strategists, we must clearly understand and demonstrate the impact of reductions and cuts. If we are effective, we'll preserve and protect school music programs for our children.

IS YOUR MUSIC PROGRAM VULNERABLE TO CUTS?

Unfortunately, the answer is generally *yes*. In today's world of precious few education dollars, music advocates *must* assume their district's music programs are competing with other programs during budget deliberations.

The most obvious sign that your music program may be in jeopardy is when you overhear—in your community, at school committee meetings, or at PTA events—any discussion about school budget issues or educational reform.

Unfortunately, cuts are often perceived as being made without prior public notice, and it may appear there is no way to prevent or reverse impending decisions. But the number-one reason that music programs are particularly vulnerable is very simple: complacency.

DANGER SIGNS OF COMPLACENCY

Do you recognize any of these signs of complacency in statements made by teachers, parents, administrators, or even by yourself? Don't wait until it's too late to notice to take action against these all too common, and very destructive, points of view: taking no action may prevent you from proactively defending and ultimately saving your school music program.

- *Denial*: People in denial generally have the belief or attitude of, "It can't/won't happen in our school district because . . ."

  "We have a very supportive administration."
  "Our district has a history of strong arts programs."
  "Our program is guaranteed by teacher prep time."
  "Our district is in a state of growth."

"Our school board members/superintendent all have children in the program."

"Something will happen to save the program."

"Our community places a high value on the arts, and music education is an important part of our identity."

"There are a number of professional musicians in our area—and many of them graduated from our district schools."

"The board/administration is just bluffing or trying to get an excess tax levy passed."

"Our district is adopting the site-based management model, and they will help prevent arts cuts."

- *Helplessness*: People who feel helpless fail to get involved because they feel powerless or failed to recognize the early signs of danger. You'll hear them say things like, "There is nothing I can do because . . ."

"The school board/superintendent will never listen to us. They just let us vent our feelings and then do what they want anyway."

"It won't help. The school board is just a rubber stamp for the administration."

"It's too late now. The decision is already made."

"There really is an enormous shortage of funding."

"We are experiencing an enrollment decline."

"Our district is going to the middle school concept and there will no longer be any room in the schedule for the arts."

"Our district is reducing the number of periods in the day."

"Our district/state is increasing the graduation requirements."

- *Apathy*: Apathy is similar to denial or helplessness and may include teachers as well as community members. Apathetic people may seem to be saying, "I don't care," but may really be saying:

"I am only a year or two from retiring anyway."

"My job won't be cut, because I have too much seniority."

"I don't have time to get involved in another project."

"I'll just find another job."

"If I let others know I care about this issue, I may end up having to serve on a committee."

"If I, as a teacher, get involved, they might cut the program out of revenge."

"There are others who will be much more able to help than I."

"If we help pass a levy, the school board/administration will just put all the money into teacher/administrator salaries anyway, and we will still lose the program."

SO, WHAT CAN YOU DO?

Take action and don't give in to complacency! In the face of what appears to be a national trend to target music programs for reduction or even elimination, it is your responsibility as a music advocate to do the following:

- Make sure you have a well-organized music coalition.
- Make sure your coalition is visibly represented at every school board meeting.
- Stay in touch with your music teachers to keep informed of what is happening in your district.

As one superintendent stated, "There is no group of people more capable of rallying immediate and effective advocacy than a well-organized music coalition!"

2

The Music Coalition

MUSIC ADVOCACY 101: DO *YOU* HAVE "THE RIGHT STUFF?"

What's the most important part of music advocacy? *You!*

There is no place where you can have more immediate political impact than in your school district. As a consultant I have not seen a music program cut when there was a well-organized local music coalition and a unified body of music teachers supplied with data relevant to the crisis. Your participation is vital to the health of your music program.

Educational institutions are, by nature and legal formation, political entities that are governed by officials who are elected to federal, state, and local office. From Washington, D.C., to your local school board, the single most significant influence on educational policy is the individual voting citizen. *Yes or no, it's all up to you!*

By participating, you cast a *yes* vote for providing music-making opportunities for students in your district. Your failure to participate is a *no* vote.

You must make the decision to become an active member of your local music coalition. The choice is yours:

- *You* are the public.
- *You* own the local public school district.
- *You* fund the local school district with your tax dollars.
- *You* elect local, state, and federal decision makers.
- *You* elect local school boards.
- *You* have the legal right and responsibility to determine educational policy.
- *You* attend meetings in the school district that establish educational policy.

- *You* hold office in the district as members of the PTA and school board.
- *You* volunteer your services to ensure quality education for your children.
- *You* hold decision makers accountable for quality education that includes music.
- *You* and other active members of your local music coalition are the ones who make sure that all decisions made by your local school district are driven by student-centered motives.

If your district doesn't have a local music coalition, it's time for *you* to become a founding organizer . . . and the sooner, the better!

YOUR LOCAL MUSIC COALITION

Why does your district need a local music coalition? Because it is the most effective way to ensure that your school district provides equal educational opportunities for all students to participate in the making of music. An effective local music coalition holds a school district accountable for its decisions.

- A local coalition places the student back to the center of the decision-making process.
- A local coalition identifies the music program as an integral part of the community.
- A local coalition affirms the music program as a unified district-wide curriculum.
- A local coalition promotes music education, not just band, choir, orchestra, or general music.
- A local coalition is a community organization that incorporates all of its constituents in the support of music making.
- A local coalition provides for bringing music into all of life.
- A local coalition puts the *public* in *public education*!

INTERNAL OR INDEPENDENT: WHICH COALITION TYPE IS BEST FOR YOUR DISTRICT?

Your music coalition may be organized as a support group within the educational system (type 1) or operate outside the district as an independent entity for the support of music within the schools (type 2). There are advantages and disadvantages of each type, as indicated in table 2.1.

Table 2.1   Comparison of Music Coalition Types

Type 1: Contained within the District	Type 2: Independent of the School District
Functions as a collaborative body within the district, potentially facilitating more cooperation within the system	May be perceived as an adversarial body, leading to potential power struggles within the community; or may function with less official regulation
May facilitate increased cooperation from administration; for example, building usage, distribution of materials, membership drives	May make it more difficult to acquire administrative cooperation
Often limits membership to parents with children currently in the program	Often limits membership to parents with children currently in the program
Tends to be oriented toward specific music performing organizations (band, orchestra, chorus)	More apt to have broad focus on music education rather than specific curricular segments
Tends to become focused on the high school	Tends to be more broad based, including representation of all levels of education
Greater turnover in leadership may lead to teacher dependency for motivation	Community ownership provides for wider leadership base and long-term participation
Oriented toward fund-raising; less focus on curricular and philosophical issues	Broader focus on all aspects of music, including philosophical and curricular issues
May lead to competition between different areas of the music program	More tendency to provide for balance between areas of the music curriculum

Districts that select the independent option often take legal steps to become recognized as a nonprofit corporation. The coalition must be structured in such a way as to provide for representation from every level of education, from each school in the district, and from the community at large. Each structure has issues that determine which form may be most successful in a specific district and that vary from district to district.

COMMITTEES WILL MAKE YOUR MUSIC COALITION MORE EFFECTIVE

The local music coalition should have a central executive committee representative of all schools in the district that provides for a balanced representation of all components of the music curriculum: band, choir, orchestra, and general music (K–12). In addition to any other basic organizational or management structures you wish to establish, I recommend that you have at least the following four committees.

Communications

Serving as the public relations arm for the music department, this committee functions as the primary means of dispersing any information related to the music program. It includes the following responsibilities.

- Recruits and activates membership

  o Provides opportunities for membership enrollment at all music functions in the district
  o Develops and maintains mailing lists
  o Develops and maintains individual and group email and telephone contact system, particularly for emergency meetings
  o Provides a visible presence at all music activities within the district

- Distributes information as a public relations entity

  o Develops, publishes, and distributes a district music newsletter
  o Develops and maintains a community music website

Administrative Liaison

This committee serves as a representative body for the exchange of information with members of the administration and school board in matters related to district policy as it affects the music program. It includes the following responsibilities.

- Represents the community as the primary advocacy body in support of music for all children in the district
- Serves as a vehicle for communication between the music faculty, administration, school board, and community in matters related to policy
- Assists or represents the music department in developing and presenting proposals related to music policy
- Acquires knowledge of administrative proposals or issues within the district that may affect the music program
- Provides representation at every school board meeting with at least one member of the committee
- Recruits, trains, supports, and elects members to the school board and legislative bodies that support music education for all children by actions that lead to specific and positive outcomes for students
- Holds public officials accountable for their decisions related to music education

Statistics and Finance

This committee serves as a representative body that fulfills the following roles.

- Represents the community in matters related to the maintenance of relevant statistical data on the music program, such as faculty issues, student participation, and economic viability
- Works with the music department, administration, and school board to develop adequate budgets for aspects of the music program that are curricular and cocurricular
- Works with the music department, administration, and school board to establish policies that restrict fund-raising to those aspects of the music program that are extracurricular or unique occasional events that may not be funded as regular line items in the curricular or cocurricular budgets, such as invitational performances at regional, national, or international events
- Works with the music department, administration, and school board to establish policies that prohibit the implementation of extra fees for curricular or cocurricular participation in music
- Manages all fund-raising activities, revenues, and specifically related expenses
- Develops an annual status report on the state of music in the school district

Philosophy and Curriculum

This committee serves as a representative body that fulfills the following roles.

- Works with the music department, administration, and school board to establish policies that facilitate music participation for all children
- Works with the music department, administration, and school board to establish a sequential written curriculum for K–12 music with learning outcomes for student achievement that are specific, achievable, measurable, and meet the minimum National Standards for Music Education as established by the Consortium of National Arts Education Associations
- Works with the music department, administration, and school board to establish a system of assessment that clearly delineates student achievement in music
- Works with music teachers to develop a system of reporting student achievement to parents that clearly delineates student achievement in music

- Works with the music department, administration, and school board to establish policies related to the evaluation of music faculty that are based on student achievement as outlined in the district music curriculum
- Works with financial and legal specialists to secure assistance in matters related to compliance with IRS or other guidelines

Finally, your coalition must be carefully structured in such a way that it does *not* become an organization for the micromanagement of the curriculum, teachers, or any particular component within the curriculum.

The Right Data = The Right Stuff

Now, assuming you have a coalition in place, do you have "the right stuff" to be effective? You'll have the most strategic power if you collect, interpret, and correctly use the right data to support your case for music.

"The right stuff" is useful for more than just defending your program. Having the right information allows you to:

- Develop annual reports on the status of the music program
- Identify issues that may be detrimental to the program
- Be specific about issues related to faculty, curriculum, student participation, and economic viability
- Identify levels of student participation and attrition
- Expand opportunities for student participation
- Justify current or new faculty positions
- Improve facilities and equipment
- Develop data related to the academic success of music students

I recommend that each local coalition have a statistics and finance committee because this information is often technical and maybe a bit complex. But once you collect and start to use this data, you'll soon realize why it's so important, and being an active participant will give you a deeper understanding of the vocabulary of the educator (see the glossary), the process of budget development, and how decisions are made.

"The Right Stuff" Adds Credibility to Your Advocacy Efforts

Approximately 35 percent of the districts with whom I have worked over the past three decades have used the right data to save their programs without a consultant site visit. Using the correct data in the right way gives music advocates more credibility with decision makers. Using "the right stuff" helps convince decision makers of the educational and economic viability of the music program. The process of collecting this basic data is described in other sections of this book.

What are *you* waiting for? It's time to gather "the right stuff" and get started!

EIGHT STRATEGIC ERRORS IN MUSIC ADVOCACY AND HOW TO CORRECT THEM

I have observed a variety of parent support groups for music throughout my consulting career and have noticed eight common mistakes made by well-meaning music advocates. While these strategic errors or misconceptions greatly limit the potential beneficial role of "booster" organizations, they can be corrected. All it takes is a commitment to reach out to others interested in our cause, some time to learn about the issues in your district, and a goal-oriented approach—in other words, all the elements of constructive, proactive music advocacy.

Strategic Error #1: Limiting Your Support Organization to a Single Local School, a Single Curricular Component, or Even a Single Year

The typical music advocacy coalition tends to be limited to parents of students currently involved in one school's music programming, for example, the Smithtown High School Band Booster's Club. Parents in a group such as this tend to concentrate on the needs in a single school or aspect of the music curriculum while losing sight of district-wide issues that may have negative effects on their children as they progress through the system. For example, what happens when your child, who loves to play clarinet in fourth grade, cannot continue making music in high school because block scheduling has been adopted in a way that makes it impossible for her to continue taking band?

This shortsighted focus can create a lack of unified support for district-wide music programs and make members competitive and divisive, while losing sight of equal access for all students. Once infighting begins, your goals can become muddied and music becomes an easier target for elimination.

Unfortunately, music teachers often prefer the single-site format because it seems easier and more convenient in the short term. Teachers who think this way may be operating out of fear and may want to discourage parents from "interfering" or micromanaging the whole program.

Solution: Invite parents from other schools to join with you to create a district-wide music coalition. Make sure you focus attention on all areas and levels of the music curriculum. Join your efforts with your music teachers and others in the community. Plan a few years ahead, creating a system of support for music education that will last long after your own children graduate. Start the ball rolling toward creating a comprehensive vision for music education in your district. Remember: You can't strategize if you don't have a plan!

Strategic Error #2: Limiting Your Support Organization to Fund-Raising Activities

Music booster organizations are a favorite of school administrations and boards. They can be very effective at fund-raising, raising additional tax support for the district. Unfortunately, overemphasis on fund-raising to the exclusion of other objectives has three major disadvantages.

1. It weakens music programs as a curricular entity, philosophically placing music in the same category as extracurricular activities like athletics.
2. It provides motivation to the administration and school board to reduce the music budget accordingly.
3. It "burns out" parents. I have actually observed several districts in which parents were told they could continue the music program—but only if they raised all the money for it, including funding the teaching positions. In at least one program, the music teacher even suggested this idea! (His spouse was employed by the music boosters at a salary of $40,000 per year.)

Solution: As a first step, coalition members need to know *why* they're raising funds. Education about music program policy issues and budgetary concerns should be a focus of your efforts. To preserve your integrity as a curricular and cocurricular entity, you should limit your fund-raising to extracurricular components of the music program. (See the sections on curricular, cocurricular, and extracurricular programs in chapter 4; also, refer to MENC's Position Statement on Fund-Raising, www.menc.org/about/view/fund-raising-position-statement.)

Strategic Error #3: Limiting Your Advocacy Activities to Music Teachers or Control by Music Teachers

Music teachers often prefer to handle advocacy efforts themselves. This may be because they sometimes see "needing" parent support as a sign of personal weakness. Teachers may also fear reprisals if they anger the administration and board. In some cases, teachers have even been ordered not to involve the parents, or told their program wouldn't be cut if they cooperated with the administration. If advocacy is limited to teachers, the administration can simply order the teachers to be quiet or be faced with job loss due to insubordination.

Solution: By law, local, state, and federal public education departments give the public the right and responsibility for educational advocacy. The legal voice of the school board is the most visible expression of this responsibility. Music advocacy, especially in times of impending cuts, must have broad community support to be most successful. Make sure parents, teachers, administrators, school board members, and, yes, even students are involved in your community's music advocacy efforts.

Strategic Error #4: Limiting Your Advocacy Efforts to Reactive Strategies

Limiting advocacy to reactive strategies may give the music coalition a public reputation as an adversarial voice of conflict. People with conflict-avoidant personalities may steer clear of participation in music advocacy because of that. Being reactive, rather than proactive, means you'll always feel—and be—"behind the eight-ball."

Solution: Make sure your coalition stays on message and presents any issues in a nonconfrontational, proactive way. Proactive strategies can help create and solidify a positive reputation for your organization, one that's collaborative, supportive, and cooperative. But, in order to be proactive, you've got to educate and inform coalition members about issues, potential threats to music program funding, staff changes, and other policy and decision-making concerns *before* music program cuts are on the table. Attend meetings, ask questions, learn to speak the language of the school board and administration, and keep your focus on building and maintaining a positive relationship.

Once you've developed a positive reputation, it's more difficult for a district to make cuts in music because they'll want to avoid offending your group. Your music coalition is simply a parent-community-teacher organization in support of music. Administrations are very aware of the need to maintain an ongoing positive relationship with music coalitions. Remember: Your music coalition is vital to them. Once a positive relationship is forged, your coalition may even be able to offer much-needed support for other proposals under district consideration.

Strategic Error #5: Procrastination

Procrastination is another form of reactive advocacy. Uninformed music advocates leave themselves no choice but to make their (often flimsy and definitely reactive) case in a moment of crisis, for instance when they learn—too late—of a potential cut or change in music programming.

Solution: Get involved before your music programs are in crisis! Monitor information on a continual basis. Once again, it's important to attend school board meetings, get to know the decision makers, and organize your coalition. But, more than that, your coalition's case for justifying music in the curriculum must always be ready, at least in the form of annual reports on the status of the music program.

In the presence of financial crisis or educational reform, you must act immediately to make sure that students who want to participate in music are not negatively impacted by any potential cut or change. Do *not* wait until after the referendum vote or final proposal for cuts or changes to make your case. It may be too late!

Strategic Error #6: Suggesting Alternate Cuts or Compromise

No one from the music coalition or teaching staff should ever make any suggestion for alternate cuts or compromise. If you do, they will be immediately accepted, and then you become responsible for them. Worse, those cuts very likely will just be added to the list of other cuts proposed. Never suggest cuts in another area of the curriculum. Leave all those decisions up to the administration and board. You are not responsible for providing them with the solution, but only advocating for the music program.

Solution: You must learn to develop impact statements that demonstrate the anticipated short- and long-term results. In other words, "If the district takes the specified action, the following will happen to the music program."

Strategic Error #7: Becoming Involved in a Battle of Music versus Athletics

Flag on the field—this is a huge mistake! It identifies you with those who philosophically characterize the music program as extracurricular.

Solution: Politely but firmly refuse to engage in this type of exchange. Keep your focus on music as curricular and cocurricular (as opposed to extracurricular) and on the importance of music within the school curriculum. Resist the temptation to compare and contrast what really amounts to comparing apples and oranges. Some like music, others prefer sports, but both have high value to students. Further, many music students will also participate in athletics.

Strategic Error #8: Resorting to Personal Attacks

Personal attacks are a desperate strategy of last resort and a glaring sign of weakness in your case. Worse, such tactics tend to establish revenge cycles that place the music curriculum on an annual cycle for continued attacks.

Solution: Make a commitment to *not* use name-calling, threats, or calls for resignations in your interactions with school board members, teachers, or school administrators, even in response to those who may attack you.

Instead, take the high road and keep your focus on the issues at hand and the needs of the students. If you see that music programs are in danger of being reduced or eliminated, study the issues, offer your help in problem-solving discussions, and present reasonable, student-centered solutions and suggestions.

YOUR MUSIC COALITION—A SPECIAL INTEREST GROUP?

Music coalitions are often accused of being special interest groups. That is true. Our special interest is preserving core curricular opportunities for all students in music. I have never met a music coalition that was advocating against math, science, reading, or any other curricular area. We become special interest groups because of the tendency of educational leaders to target music programs as their first avenue of attack in a financial crisis or act of educational reform.

ADVOCACY AND THE MUSIC STUDENT

Under the right circumstances, music students may play an extremely critical role in creating, maintaining, and energizing support for local music programs. After all, they speak from a very personal musical perspective: They are the ones who are most directly impacted when school music programs are cut or eliminated. How can students take effective action? Here are a few examples of the power and potential of creative student advocacy.

- *Scenario #1:* The board had scheduled a meeting to decide the fate of the music program. A number of cuts had already been proposed by the administration. The auditorium was filled to standing-room-only capacity; no one was ever able to count the number of people outside. A high school student stepped forward to speak on the open microphone. He followed protocol: "My name is _____. I have nothing to say. I just brought my trumpet and would like to play 'Taps' for the music program." His musical performance was the most moving and effective "speech" of the evening.
- *Scenario #2:* In another district, the music program was targeted for complete elimination. Several high school students had the idea to obtain a legal parade permit. In cooperation with the local radio station, they arranged to have Sousa marches played for the duration of the parade. Down Main Street they marched, in full uniform—no instruments—only boom boxes! The message was very clear.

- *Scenario #3:* In a third district, the elementary band program was in jeopardy. As people filed into the school auditorium for the board meeting, the entire high school marching band performed on stage. As they began to play, band members gradually left the stage leaving only a remnant of the former group. The demonstration effectively portrayed the potential demise of the high school program, a direct result of eliminating the elementary feeder program.

The Power of Creative Action—and Silence

Student advocates have used many other creative means to convey the importance of music programs and dramatically illustrate what would happen if funding were cut. Keep in mind that any presentations at board meetings should be brief. Select only one or two speakers. Write out any presentations and rehearse them. Make sure musical performances are top-notch. Avoid repetition and overkill, and remember the power of silence as you create your presentations.

Here are a few more examples of effective actions that music students can easily take.

- Playing outdoor or indoor concerts before board meetings
- Attending board meetings in uniform, but remaining silent
- Presenting petitions and/or brief accompanying speeches
- Developing music advocacy strategies as an assignment for political science classes

A Note of Caution: Danger Ahead!

Student groups should only take action after careful consideration. While you are planning your actions, imagine worst-case scenarios and negative results, as well as your intended successes: even the best laid plans may backfire. You certainly don't want to alienate people or establish revenge cycles that place your program in annual jeopardy.

Some additional words of warning and advice:

- *No music teachers or parents should be responsible for instigating student actions.* Aside from the fact that teachers risk being reprimanded or dismissed, using adults as spokespeople undermines the credibility of the student action.
- Students should seek adult counsel to make sure that actions they want to take are legal.
- No actions should embarrass or attack any individuals or a specific group.

- Don't get into a contest that pits music programs against athletics programs. This can have the extremely detrimental effect of incorrectly categorizing music as an extracurricular activity.
- Make sure your actions are age-appropriate for the students involved.

Finally, from my personal perspective, one of the most effective, long-term, and empowering actions that students can easily take is to bring their parent(s) with them to school board meetings.

3

The School System

DECISION MAKING: COLLABORATION VERSUS POWER

In the ideal model, the law constructs a system in which the various players collaborate to make the district work for the benefit of the students. The system is referred to as public education because the public owns it, pays for it, and has the right and responsibility to determine educational policy for its children through its elected board.

The school board is a public servant acting as community liaison, establishing policy, and evaluating the system through its administration to ensure that community wishes are fulfilled. It is the voice of the people.

The administration is a servant to the community and board and has the primary responsibility of carrying out community-established policy and making sure that each member of the educational community understands and does the same.

The best decisions are made when the most student-centered people (the parents or community) are involved. The advantage of a collaborative decision-making process that involves the community is that the community is the primary entity that can keep the decision-making process focused on learning—the student-centered issue. A collaborative decision-making process also frees the administration and board from the full political responsibility for a decision.

In the typical school district, the normal practice of decision making is based on a power structure; that is, whoever assumes power has the most influence on the results.

- The administration makes centralized or site-based recommendations and decisions as empowered by the board.

- The board approves or disapproves, often appearing as "rubber stamps" because no one else gives them any information.
- Depending on the amount of power associated with a particular union, teachers may or may not be involved in the process; usually music teachers are not involved.

This decision-making process tends to be adult-centered because the community is either intentionally excluded (your participation is not wanted or valued), or excluded by default (no one shows up at board meetings). Without the involvement of the community, decisions tend to be driven by whatever adult issues are present, such as salary, teaching schedules, educational reforms, or money.

DECISIONS: ADULT- OR STUDENT-CENTERED?

Since first becoming a consultant-advocate for music education, I have asked over thirty thousand teachers, parents, and school administrators to define the mission of education. In over 99 percent of the responses, adults define the mission as "teaching or educating children." Asked the same question, the majority of students respond that the mission of education is "learning." It is my observation that this is the number-one issue in education today. No decision should ever be made without someone asking: *"What will the short- and long-term impacts of this decision be on the students?"*

Federal mandates, the demand for increasing test scores, the shortage of funding for public education, and a variety of other issues often convey an environment of negativism toward public education and in particular the public school educator. Even in states or districts that have demonstrated standards of excellence in student achievement there is often the presence of a public attitude that assumes, "Since there are problems in education somewhere they must be just as bad in our district, too."

This crisis of negativism places the educators in the position of constantly defending their roles as administrators or teachers. The need to demonstrate administrative leadership or skills as a teacher can drive the decision makers to operate out of personal need. The need for self-preservation politicizes the decision-making process and can lead to conflict (power struggles) between administrators, school boards, teachers, and the community. Student learning can become a secondary issue.

While public education exists for learning, the decision makers in any school district are adults. Adults tend to make decisions based upon the perspective their position gives them on any issue. Administrators solve problems from an administrative perspective: budgets, staffing, public relations, and keeping teachers happy. Teachers solve problems from a teaching perspective: class size, student loads, salaries and benefits, and keeping parents happy.

When the mission of education is perceived as *teaching* or *educating*, adult-centered issues may drive the decision-making process. The influence of adult-centered issues in the decision-making process is often subtle. At other times it is blatantly obvious. Somehow educators seem to have adopted the concept that if we solve the issues that surface related to our job conditions, we have improved the learning of our students. Consequently decisions tend to be made that resolve adult needs but do not necessarily improve learning.

Some examples based on actual school districts may serve to illustrate the problem.

- *Example #1:* The school district is in a financial crisis. The administrators decide that all students will be required to schedule a one-period study hall as part of their six-period day. This would facilitate the elimination of a significant number of teachers and place 250 students per hour in one large room with a single supervisor. (See "The Study Hall Game" in chapter 8.)

  While the district is in a financial crisis, further research into the situation reveals that there is a music teacher the administration had wanted to fire for several years. The financial crisis provides the perfect opportunity. The district mandates the elimination of 50 percent of the entire music teaching staff in order to go deep enough into the seniority tract to eliminate that teacher. The decision to require each student to schedule one study period per day was primarily to provide space for those students who would no longer be able to take music.

  The result: When these facts are revealed to the parents, the administration rescinds their recommendation and reinstates the music program.

- *Example #2:* Elementary schools in the district are overcrowded, but building a new school is not an option. Changing attendance boundaries or areas would solve the problem, but is an extremely volatile political issue. The district decides to approach the problem with "educational reform." They will adopt a middle school structure of education.

  The result: The sixth graders are moved into the old junior high facilities. The names are changed, but little else. They may add an exploratory wheel in which student take a greater variety of subjects or activities, or even make a few other changes. General music is reduced from a full year to a six-week exploratory format. Band, choir, and orchestra are reduced from daily instruction to every other day to facilitate more exploratory classes, and music teachers are replaced with exploratory teachers. Lessons and elementary (grade 5 and lower) beginning instrumental instruction are eliminated. Elementary classroom teachers are happier because the "pull-out" lessons are gone. In essence, the district has moved students from overcrowded schools to those with more room (changed boundaries) under a guise of educational reform, but in reality little has changed other than the location.

- *Example #3:* The district hires a new administrator who decides to investigate various alternatives of educational reform. The district decides to adopt block scheduling.

  The result: Students lose eight weeks of instructional time per course. The new administrator demonstrates leadership skill as an "agent of change." (Note: In every district that has consulted me about block schedule as educational reform, there has been a new administrator leading the change.) (See "Scheduling" in chapter 7.)

- *Example #4:* In a small district, the administration and guidance counselors are working out the class schedule for the coming year. One major issue seems to be in the way of completing the process: all the coaches (including the high school principal) participate in an amateur basketball league. Their schedules have all been arranged so that they have the last hour of the day free in order to facilitate team practice in the gym. The problem: There are no other teachers available to supervise study hall during the last period.

  The result: Although the band director is voluntarily teaching band lessons during his prep hour, it is decided that the only logical action is to eliminate lessons and assign study hall supervision to the band director.

- *Example #5:* One music teacher is asking another about the cuts to the music program in their district. The second teacher responded, "We lost a couple of positions, but we are still okay."

  The result: In other words, the teacher is saying, "I managed to save my job!" Now what is the primary concern of that teacher? Obviously, he cares more about the job than the students or the program!

PUTTING THE STUDENT FIRST IS THE KEY!

When you approach music education from a student's perspective, everything shifts in a subtle, yet very significant, way. This is one area where advocates for music education have a crucial role to play. If adults who are decision makers aren't able or willing to shift their perspective—from "teaching" to "learning"—it's easy to see how school music programs end up as prime targets for cuts.

Your message will only be well received if you are able to convey how crucial it is to put students first. Music advocacy is most effective when it is:

- Proactive and collaborative. A music coalition must work together with music teachers and administrators to make sure official policy includes curricular music standards.
- About learning. Remember, music education is not about what adults teach, it's about what students learn.
- Focused on the students. Every decision should be prefaced with the question, "What will the long-term effect be on students?"

On the flip side, music advocacy may be perceived as negative, and therefore be less effective, when it is:

- Reactive or adversarial, to save a program that is proposed for reduction or elimination
- About money and raising taxes
- About conflict and power—the administration versus the board versus the teachers versus the community
- About teachers—job conditions, pay, or benefits
- About saving jobs—losing individuals, not positions or curriculum
- About adults, or focused on anything other than learning

Basically, a successful music advocacy campaign comes down to two primary components:

- A well-organized music coalition
- Strategic use of the right information

A Little Advice

There are many ways you can work to head off a potentially destructive situation. Just keep in mind that being an effective advocate for music education is about music for students—all students! Music advocacy is based on the belief that making music is essential to learning, the enjoyment of life, and the preservation of culture. Being effective as a music advocate means focusing at least some of your energy on expansion of existing programs and development of new ones, not only on defending music programs against cuts or threats of elimination. As an advocate for music education, you are part of a long and proud tradition of putting students first. Together we can keep the focus on what's most important—students making music!

THE SCHOOL BOARD

Various titles may be given to the body of individuals who govern the decision-making process in a school district. By law they have one basic responsibility: to establish policy. They are not in a position legally or otherwise to micromanage the educational system. School boards that attempt to do so can become one of the greatest detriments to successful management of a school system. There are two basic types of school boards. The first, and most typical, is *elected* directly by the vote of the people.

The elected school board is the legal voice of the people. However, it is often the case that these elected individuals, often highly gifted in their own occupational fields, become less effective in the educational system. This may be because they are not familiar with the language of the educator or the system, or that the public fails to maintain its involvement with the school board once it has been elected.

The second category is the board of education that is *appointed* by other elected officials. The disadvantages here become obvious. Typically this type may be more obligated to make its decisions to please those who appointed it than the general public. This in turn means that the members are further removed from the direct influence of the public, and that in order to influence student-centered decision making the public must broaden its political strategies of influence to more constituencies. In such cases, the public may feel so removed from the realm of political influence that it completely withdraws from the process.

In either case, once the public is excluded or chooses to be excluded from the decision-making process, the school board is often accused of being a rubber stamp for administrative proposals. What other choice do they have if no one else gives them any information? In my experience as a board member and a consultant I have found that most school board members are quite competent, understand human resource issues, and are capable of making reasonably sound economic decisions. Further, it is my experience that most board members will side with the public position, particularly if the public stance is based upon a presentation that is rational and supported by a broad constituency within the community.

When working with a school board to effect positive decisions for music education, here are some practical suggestions.

- Be present at board meetings.
- Be involved in other activities of the district, such as committee memberships that establish your credibility.
- Elect school board members who understand the importance of music making in the core curriculum.
- Work to establish positive relationships with all board members, even

those who may not appear to support music education.
- Strengthen relationships with those who support music education.
- Cultivate relationships with those who may be neutral.
- Be careful not to offend or personally attack those who may appear to be the "no" voters.
- Remember that you only need a majority vote in any decision.

CENTRAL AND SITE-BASED MANAGEMENT

Your effectiveness as a music advocate will improve with greater insight into the centralized and site-based administration systems, two well-defined layers of school district management and responsibility. The more you understand the various lines of authority between (and within) these two levels of power, the more effective you may be in working within the systems established in your district.

When reading, keep in mind that management roles may vary greatly from district to district based upon state laws and student population size. For instance, in a small school district, all management responsibilities may be covered by the central administration only; in others, where there are several schools within a large district, the central administration may delegate increased responsibilities to individual school principals.

Central Management: The Hub of the Wheel

In centralized management, levels of authority or responsibility are assigned by law or district policy to the chief executive of the school district. The chief executive, usually a superintendent, has various levels of support staff to assist in the day-to-day operations of the district. In descending order of authority, these support staff may include, among other personnel:

- Assistants
- Directors
- Supervisors
- Coordinators

Each position has a specific job description, level of authority, and responsibility for evaluation of subordinate personnel. Keep in mind that the status of the music program is often directly related to the authority level of personnel in charge of that area. For example, if the music department is under the authority of a director, music programs may gain greater budgetary security than when placed under the authority of a lower-level coordinator. (See "The Music Administrator" in chapter 4.)

The Central Administration and the Board of Education

The effectiveness of the operation of a school district is often directly related to the relationship between the board and superintendent. Contact with other members of the central administration will depend on the issue(s) being discussed and the management style of the superintendent. In my experience, the most effective administrators are highly skilled at staff evaluation and collaborative decision making.

Giving power to the various levels of administrative decision making does not remove the board of education's responsibility to ensure a music education for all children. The board has the right and responsibility to establish policies such as, "All children shall have equal access to a music education in all grades." It may further define this policy to conform to community expectations.

The Central Administration and the District Budget

The central administration also manages any line items in the budget that fall under its supervision. In a typical music program this includes any music teachers assigned as part of the negotiated teacher contract for release or pre-paratory time (e.g., elementary general music specialists) and itinerant teach-ers with multiple school assignments (e.g., elementary instrumental music). Itemized or publicized budget cuts that specifically identify aspects of the music program normally only appear at the central administration level.

During the budgetary decision-making process, the central administra-tion establishes the staffing ratio. The staffing ratio relates directly to the number of teaching positions available to a single school site. (See discus-sion of FTE and SFR in chapter 8.)

Site-Based Management: The Local Layer of Authority

Site administrators (principals) and supporting staff are responsible for decisions at individual schools in the district. The various levels of person-nel are also provided with specific job descriptions and levels of authority. In descending order these include the following:

- Assistants
- Guidance counselors
- Directors
- Department chairs or other personnel as determined by the district

Site-Based Management and Budget Autonomy

The principal and staff are responsible to the central administration as deter-mined by the district. However, once the staffing ratios are assigned, site administrators generally have autonomous decision-making authority. In other words, if the central administration determines that the size of classes will be increased, the site administrator will make decisions regarding staff cuts.

I refer to these as hidden cuts because budgetary line items rarely include the term *music* in the list of impending cuts. However, the music staff or budget may be significantly affected by those local site decisions. Music advocates must become aware of all the budgetary line items in their district that include music.

WHERE DOES THE TRUE POWER EXIST?

Periodically there are shifts in management philosophy that place more emphasis on site-based management. This educational reform movement is intended to facilitate increased community input and produce a more collaborative, student-centered decision-making process at the local level. This concept works most effectively in a system with balanced representation from the community and professional educators—including music advocates, of course.

Site-based management is diminished, or even dangerous, when the membership displays curricular bias or cronyism, or is dominated by the personal philosophy of an individual administrator.

To keep the focus on the importance of music programs—regardless of whether your district places more emphasis on a centralized or site-based management style—your local music coalition must be visible. As an advocate, your presence must be felt at both central and site administrative levels, as well as at school board meetings, where ultimately the final authority rests. If not, our music programs will be in constant threat of reduction or elimination.

WHO REALLY CALLS THE SHOTS?

An ideal decision-making process is collaborative, with all members of the community actively involved. The advantage of a collaborative, community-based decision-making process is that it keeps the focus squarely on learning and the needs of students. A truly collaborative process also frees the administration and board from political responsibility for any decision because of broad-based community ownership.

The welfare of the students should always be the driving force for every decision made by the district. When the flow of power starts in the community and then moves through the board to the administration and educational institution, student-centered decisions are made.

I've noticed that the further removed decision makers are from daily contact with students, the greater their tendency to base decisions upon adult-centered issues such as balancing the budget, educational reforms, or teaching schedules. You can easily see, then, why the community—and especially your local music coalition—has such a key role in advocating for student-centered decisions and the support of music in the curriculum.

Exert the "3 Vs"—Be Visible, Be Verbal, and Vote!

Who really influences school administrators and board members to listen to the needs and interests of students? Voters! Regardless of how strong your case is to save (or build) your music program, the administration and board must see and hear from voters to persuade them to decide in your favor. Assuming your music coalition has an administrative liaison committee, use it to keep open lines of communication with the board and administration at all levels of decision-making.

The board is the appropriate and most effective place to make your visible, verbal, and voting presence felt. The educational system is based upon a political structure and process. It is a product of public elections at federal, state, and local levels and, not surprisingly, is a system that tends to focus on adult-centered issues. The largest single factor affecting decision makers is their perception of prevailing public opinion. If the majority of your school board's constituents visibly support a strong music program, they (as your elected officials) will be less likely to weaken or eliminate it. *Remember: Process is politics!*

Unfortunately, the practice of making decisions in a typical school district tends to be based more on who has been given—or has assumed—the right and responsibility to make them. This may be determined by the relative strength of personalities or organized groups within the educational structure, or by the adoption of an authoritarian concept of administration. In such cases, any one or all of the following situations may be evident:

- The administration makes centralized and/or local site-based recommendations and decisions as empowered by the board. This can happen by intent or default, and often includes various assumptions of autonomy in the process.
- The board normally gives rubber-stamp approval to administrative recommendations or decisions. This may occur because no one besides the administration has offered information or input, and those recommendations may then be perceived as the only possible solution.
- Teachers may or may not be involved in the process, depending on the

amount of power associated with a particular teacher organization. Usually music teachers are not involved. If music teachers do become directly involved, their actions may be interpreted as a conflict of interest or insubordination.

- The decision-making process is adult centered. This can happen because the community is either intentionally excluded (your participation is not wanted or valued), or excluded by default (no one shows up at board meetings). With little or no community involvement, decisions tend to be driven by adult issues (salaries, benefits, teaching loads or schedules, educational reform, money, etc.).
- Such decisions are often power-based. Whoever has the power—or claims it—gets the decision to go their way. If community members are not active participants, students often lose.

THE POWERFUL INFLUENCE OF UNITY

The single most important reason for organizing a unified local music coalition—made up of parents, community members, and teachers representing band, choir, orchestra, and general music concerns in equal measure—is to broaden your political power base. A single body presenting a unified voice speaks much louder than any small group of parents. A unified music coalition is usually far more effective than any of its subgroups.

In the process of making any decision about school budgets, one question must always be asked: *"What will the short- and long-term impacts of this decision be on the students in the district?"*

As music advocates, it's up to us to get, and sometimes even provide, the answers—before decisions are made.

If you show up and take part of the process, you'll find out who really calls the shots. The answer might surprise you, because it could—and should—be "advocates for students." That means *you* and the other members of your local music coalition!

Remember: "The decision belongs to those who show up!"
—Dr. Dennis R. Morrow, superintendent

4

The Profession

MUSIC: CURRICULAR, COCURRICULAR, OR EXTRACURRICULAR? YES!

Confused? That's not surprising, since music programs can, in fact, be curricular, cocurricular, and extracurricular. Lack of clarity about this issue is one of the main reasons so many music programs come under constant attack.

Legal Definitions Vary Widely

State laws are inconsistent in relation to music education. Legal definitions tend to be unclear and may combine or interchange terms. This means your local school district administration or school board may have little legal guidance regarding the academic status of the music curriculum.

State laws may even completely ignore the status of music education or mandate only certain (usually very broad) standards. For example, the state may fund positions for band or choir teachers, but not orchestra. In other cases the state may provide detailed standards that are merely classified as "guidelines," meaning they provide no legal basis for including music in the curriculum. In nearly every case, the local district administration has great flexibility in how to interpret the laws related to the music curriculum and music staffing.

Here are definitions of each of the three classifications commonly used for music education programs.

Curricular Music Education

Curricular activities are primarily cognitive events, not merely activities. They contribute substantially to students' social, academic, intellectual, expressive, and communicative development. Music education is also curricular for some very practical reasons:

- Music classes, including rehearsals, are held during the regular school day. This is one reason why it is vital to maintain performance rehearsals during regular class time. Once a performance program is moved outside the regular schedule, it becomes extracurricular and vulnerable to cuts, since extracurricular programs are generally the first to go.
- The regular salaries of music teachers are funded by the same budget as other academic teachers.
- Music teachers have a full-time equivalent (FTE) value that is similar to that of other classroom teachers. In fact, music ensemble teachers, especially at the secondary level, usually have a greater financial value to the district because they teach larger classes.
- All curricular and cocurricular music courses should receive academic credit.

Curricular examples of music include: (nonperformance) classroom general music, music theory and history, music appreciation, and rehearsals of music performing organizations in preparation for cocurricular concerts including the content and process of learning about the music as stated in the fulfillment of competencies outlined in the curriculum.

Cocurricular Music Education

Some aspects of the academic music curriculum occur outside of the regular school day, such as the musical performance as a final exam in the form of a public concert. Though a primary function of the concert is public demonstration of skills acquired during classroom learning, these concerts often have public relations or public service value. These activities are or should be funded as part of the regular salary of music performance teachers. They are cocurricular.

Cocurricular examples of music include: Band, choir, and orchestra concerts.

Extracurricular Music Education

Whenever the performance of any district music organization is motivated primarily by public service or public relations, that organization becomes (temporarily) extracurricular.

Nearly all extracurricular events are held outside the normal school day on evenings and weekends. Some organizations exist primarily for public service or public relations; these should be considered totally extracurricular, and funded as such. Music teachers should receive additional stipends for supervision of extracurricular activities.

Unfortunately, music educators are most visible to the public in their extracurricular role. If music educators make no distinction between curricular, cocurricular, and extracurricular aspects of the music curriculum, the general assumption is often that music educators and music programs are all extracurricular.

Extracurricular examples of music include: Performance at any event that is not a specific learner outcome of the music curriculum, such as athletic events, service clubs, and civic events.

Where Does Confusion Surface and Create Problems?

The confusion about classifying music programs surfaces in differing perspectives on four major areas of music education:

1. *Academic status*: Educators, administrators, and school boards differ on how to interpret the academic status of a music education program within the framework of state law. Sometimes cocurricular and extracurricular may be the same, but distinguished from curricular. In other cases, the three categories are interchanged or even interpreted as identical. In my experience, legal definitions are rarely considered other than to provide a vehicle for moving music higher on priority lists for "make budget cuts here first."

2. *Allocation of funds*: Music programs can appear as line items in all three budgetary categories. This is particularly true when directors of music ensembles receive extracurricular stipends for music performances that are funded out of the same budget categories as nonmusic activities perceived as extracurricular, such as athletics. To add further confusion, sometimes the music performance curriculum is even governed by the same state agency that oversees athletic competitions.

3. *Philosophical debates*: Music educators themselves may disagree about which category or categories best define their music programs. There are various philosophical positions related to differences between those who emphasize music performance versus those who emphasize music education. The issues are similar to those that occur between educators surrounding athletics versus physical education. In addition, there are opposing philosophical views regarding music education for all versus advancement of the gifted or elite; as one music teacher

described it, "We start 500 new students in band and orchestra each year. By the time they reach high school, we have it 'weeded down' to the best 50!"

4. *No SAM*: I've worked as music educator and consultant with over 400 districts, few of which had a *written, sequential curriculum with specific, achievable, and measurable (SAM) goals*. Several districts have had well-developed curricular components, some with relatively complete written documents. However, when such documents existed, one or more of the following deficiencies were evident:

- Curricular statements were written as teaching objectives, not learner outcomes.
- None of the music teachers were able to locate a copy of the curriculum; most ignored it and continued to teach to their own standards and expectations.
- Few teachers had given any consideration at all to the National Standards for Music Education.
- There were no learner outcomes defining what students should know and be able to do upon completion of their music education— and no standard or consistent system to assess what students were accomplishing.
- Without a student assessment system, school districts could not demonstrate the legitimacy of music education as a curricular or academic entity to their administration and school board.

What Can You *Do* about All This?

The first step is to define the three classifications—curricular, cocurricular, and extracurricular—as you define your district philosophy. Policies will be based upon these definitions; they are the foundation on which you will establish the academic legitimacy of music education with your administration and board.

Until we as music educators and music advocates take the lead and establish clear definitions and assessment systems, music education programs will continue to be viewed as non-curricular and therefore expendable.

I recommend the following course of action:

- Identify every course, performing organization, and performance in your music education program as curricular, cocurricular, or extracurricular. Specify that curricular and cocurricular music programs and music staffing be funded under the regular salary and budget line items for music performance and music education. Define staffing and programmatic expenses for extracurricular music activities as separate line items.

- Submit your document with appropriate definitions to your school board for adoption as official district policy.
- Establish a system to assess student achievement. This will require planning, input, data collection, and consistent written documentation from all music educators in the district.
- Submit the curriculum and assessment documents to your school board for adoption as official district policy.

Once the music curriculum is defined and established as official district policy, this foundation will help preserve your program in times of budgetary crisis. More importantly, in the long run, it will help you protect, strengthen, and perhaps even expand music programming and student participation in music making.

THE ROLE OF ASSESSMENT IN ADVOCACY

Contributed by Stephen Benham, Ph.D.

In the section above, we discuss the status of music programs as curricular, cocurricular, or extracurricular, emphasizing that the best scenario is a curricular music program. An essential part of achieving that status is the existence of a useable, practical, and adaptable curriculum for systematically guiding student learning, ensuring long-term program success, and generating administrative and community support. The existence of a curriculum, however, isn't enough. Assessment must be a central consideration in curriculum development and reform.

The ultimate goal of assessment is twofold: first, assessment should *reveal and inform* teachers, parents, and other interested parties as to what students are learning. Second, assessment should *guide* teaching practice, curricular reform, and the day-to-day activities taking place in the rehearsal or classroom.

Understanding Assessment

Assessment is a two-part process that includes both the measurement of student aptitude and achievement and the evaluation of that information. Measuring and evaluating student *achievement* is separate from the measurement of *aptitude*. While these terms are related (i.e., achievement should reflect student aptitude or potential), how a student performs on a playing test doesn't necessarily demonstrate his or her potential in that particular musical skill.

Aptitude tests are crucial in determining what student learning needs are (e.g., if a student will need additional instruction in rhythm because his or her rhythmic aptitude is not as high as other students') and to be sure that students are achieving at their potential. Aptitude testing provides baseline information for teachers to understand individual student learning needs, and further, readiness for beginning a musical instrument. Aptitude is about potential to learn music, while achievement is about what has already been learned in music. Finally, assessment should be used to ensure that students with high music aptitude, who might otherwise be overlooked during the recruitment process, are included into the program.[1]

The best teachers assess student aptitude *and* achievement, and use this information to revise lesson plans, teaching habits, instructional delivery, or curricular goals. These teachers use assessment as a strategic and intentional means of guiding student learning. They are committed to assessment as a process *and* a practice.

For these teachers, assessment is habitual. They have a comprehensive approach to assessment that includes everything from the instantaneous decision making that takes place during the rehearsal to measuring student aptitude and achievement at crucial points throughout the program.

Finally, these teachers include students in the assessment process, helping students and parents to focus on specific learning needs and on setting goals for future growth. In this way, assessment is a *constructive* rather than *punitive* practice. As mentioned earlier in this book, when parents and administrators see that teachers have student learning as the primary goal for the music program, and when this is reflected in assessment practice, *their support for that teacher and program is greatly increased.*

Where Assessment Goes Wrong

When secondary uses of assessment, such as assigning grades or determining seating within an ensemble, are the main practice of the teacher, problems are likely to occur. These uses are inherently subjective and do not necessarily reflect student learning. This is particularly true when grades and seating are based on nonmusical items, such as attendance or attitude.

Using assessment primarily for these reasons unfortunately weakens the academic status of the class and opens the teacher and program to accusations of favoritism, elitism, and subjectivity. Unfortunately, this can actually have a negative effect on community perception, and actually decrease public support for the program.

---

1. For a full discussion of music aptitude and aptitude testing, see E. E. Gordon, "All About Audiation and Music Aptitudes," *Music Educators Journal* 86 (1999): 41–44; and E. E. Gordon, *Music Aptitude and Related Tests: An Introduction* (Chicago: GIA Publications, 2001).

In spite of all of these challenges, the best teachers are still committed to the assessment process.

Problems in Assessment Practice

Music teachers express multiple reasons for why assessment is not a routine part of their music program. These include rapidly changing policies and mandates, inconsistent terminology, lack of teacher training and understanding, previous negative experience with assessment processes, lack of funding, perceived irrelevance of mandated assessment procedures (one-size-fits-all approaches), belief that music as an art form should not be measured, fear of how assessment results will be used (either for themselves or for the students), and, of course, *the lack of a curriculum.*

However, the mere existence of a curriculum by itself is not enough if systematic, intentional, and strategic assessment is not taking place at the same time. Assessment and curriculum are closely linked. A curriculum that is not assessed is essentially meaningless. Likewise, assessment without a clear direction, plan, or course (i.e., a curriculum) is incomplete and is frequently abandoned. The curriculum should be flexible enough to respond to the information that is obtained through assessment, a flexibility that includes a willingness to revise daily lesson plans or rewrite a district curriculum based on where students really are!

Teachers who resist assessing student performance for any of the reasons above, or refuse changing and improving their instruction based on assessment feedback, not only reflect poorly on our profession, but also call into question the validity, meaning, and role of the music program in the core curriculum. If music education is going to continue to be a part of a child's education, we need to develop an apologetic for music that is defined by musical principles and best practice, and reinforced by research. This includes the process of assessment.

Questions Every Music Teacher Should Ask about Assessment

As you reflect on your current assessment practice, consider the points and questions listed below. These issues are central to reforming assessment practice in music education and differentiating music education from other academic subjects. An answer of "no" to any of the questions reveals flaws in assessment practice.

- In any music class, no matter how much we attempt to homogenize our groups, there will be a range of abilities and talents—that is the nature of human development.
- *Do your assessment procedures reflect this characteristic of student achievement?*

- If music is a unique subject and different from math, science, reading, and so forth, it should be evaluated on uniquely musical things.
- *Do your assessment procedures demonstrate that music is a unique activity? Do you evaluate students on musical skills and knowledge or on nonmusical factors?*
- A student's learning is gauged over time and cannot be adequately captured in an isolated event.
- *Do your assessment procedures reflect student development and progress against short- and long-term goals? Do you maintain a portfolio or record of student learning over time, or do you only measure single events?*
- What is the stated purpose, most frequently, of grading? What should it be? To assist the teacher in understanding how to improve instruction. A test that results in all "A" grades for the class only tells the teacher that the material on the test was too easy. Likewise, a test that was too difficult, and results in all "F" grades, is not an adequate measurement because it doesn't help improve instruction.
- *Is the primary purpose of your evaluation systems to assign grades, or do you conduct evaluation to see what your students do not know, in addition to what they do know?*
- Measurement and evaluation should be designed to assist students in understanding their own progress and development.
- *Do you conduct assessment in a way that helps guide student development and self-understanding? Are your assessments focused more on process or on product?*
- Assessment procedures should be thoughtful and intentional. Meaningless measurement does not help the student or the teacher. It is necessary to establish goals, objectives, outcomes, and standards to assist the teacher in the evaluation process. The absence of a written curriculum calls into question the validity of the program.
- *Does your program have clearly established learning outcomes (musicianship, technique, and other related knowledge) against which you conduct regular assessment? Does assessment occur on a regular basis, or is it conducted in a haphazard manner? Do you have a curriculum or course of study that is usable and practical?*
- Your system of evaluation reflects what you believe about children, music, and music education; this is clear to the students, parents, and community as a whole!
- *Do you demonstrate to students, parents, teachers, and administrators that music is a serious subject because you have a clearly established evaluation system, or does the lack of regular and intentional evaluation reveal that music is somehow lesser than the other core subjects? Are you in danger of being marginalized because your program doesn't comply with standards?*

Practical Solutions for Implementing or Revising Assessment Practice

A full discussion of music assessment is beyond the scope of this book, so I strongly recommend that you refer to the bibliography for additional materials and references. A full glossary of terminology related to assessment is also included in the back of the book. However, I want to provide some practical first steps that you may want to consider.

- Be proactive: Plan ahead, develop goals before you begin the year, and determine *how* and *when* you will assess student progress against those goals; be sure that goals are specific, achievable, and measurable (SAM).
- Be clear: Develop policies that are easily understood by students, parents, and administrators.
- Be consistent and fair: Specific goals may vary for students based on individual aptitude and achievement, but teacher conduct in implementing assessment practice is crucial to long-term success.
- Be a *music* educator first: Emphasize musical behaviors over extramusical factors; music performance including executive technique, musicianship, and artistic skills and knowledge should be the priority; expectations for good attitude and attendance, though important, are not unique to music!
- Be comprehensive: Collect a variety of data including performance samples, student compositions, analysis and critique of performance, and written theory; use both formative and summative procedures.[2]
- Be relevant: Make sure that students know that you review what they do and use information obtained in assessment to improve their learning experience; make sure that they see the value of the process; include students in evaluating their own work.
- Be realistic: You know how much time you have and how much instruction you lose to everything from classroom interruptions to illness and school cancellations; start slowly and achieve success in small steps.
- Be an example: Offer students the opportunity to assess what works and what doesn't work for them in the classroom; find out from parents how their children learn best; by demonstrating that you are assessing your own teaching and continuing to learn, you set an excellent example for students.
- Be willing to experiment—and fail: As you develop your ideas about assessment, don't hesitate trying out new ideas as pilot projects in the classroom; share what worked and what didn't work with the students; and remember—not all assessment has to be graded!

---

2. See glossary for definitions of formative and summative assessment.

Examples of Flawed and Exemplary Rubrics

The bibliography contains excellent resources for the music teacher for designing rubrics and other types of assessment tools. However, I wanted to briefly show three types of rubrics in this section. The first example (figure 4.1), unfortunately, is found all too frequently in the music classroom. The second and third examples (figures 4.2 and 4.3) are both positive, focused, and comprehensive assessment practices.[3]

Comments/Flaws: In figure 4.1 grades are not clearly explained, the numerical system is confusing, the majority of items listed are not related to musical outcomes, and even the categories may be interpreted as having multiple meanings. The addition of explanations for what the numbers 1, 2, and 3 mean doesn't really help. For example, what does "1" in attendance mean? The student was *always* there? The student was *always* absent? The teacher also varied from the numerical system in the performance category.

Comments: The scale in figure 4.3 provides different categories for different skills. The form is clear and concise, with categories that represent specific and unique musical skills. The definition of rating scale points (see next section) is a crucial part of this rating scale. Without an explanation of what the points mean, the teacher is less likely to be consistent, and students and parents are less likely to understand what the numbers mean.

Name_____School_____
Instrument_____Teacher _____Grade_

Category	Grade (1, 2, or 3)
Attendance	1
Attitude	1
Effort	2
Materials	3
Practice Card	2
Performance	1.5

1—Always
2—Sometimes
3—Never

Figure 4.1.   Flawed Rating Scale: Summary Music Class Assessment Form—Any Level

3. All examples taken from S. Benham, "Musical Assessment as an Impetus for Strategic, Intentional, and Sustainable Growth in the Instrumental Classroom," in *The Practice of Assessment in Music Education*, ed. Timothy Brophy (Chicago: GIA Publications, 2009). Used by permission.

Criteria	Yes/No
Body is balanced and centered over feet	
Body is lengthened	
Instrument falls naturally between shoulder and chin in playing position	
Instrument is angled to provide ease of access for bowing and fingering	
Elbow falls over left foot, under instrument	
Left hand is balanced on arm (i.e., does not lean back or forward, providing access for finger extensions both directions, plus ease of motion for vibrato)	
Hand is angled to allow all fingers to contact string while maintaining curved knuckles	
Hand contacts neck slightly above base knuckle of index finger	
Total	

Figure 4.2. Exemplary Rating Scale—Focused
Left Hand: Instrument and Arm Placement Rating Scale—Additive (8 points)

City High School
Student Performance Rating Sheet

Name_____Date_____

Instrument_____Music Selection(s)_____

Fundamentals:	1	2	3	4
Right Hand Position	☐	☐	☐	☐
Left Hand Position	☐	☐	☐	☐
Posture/Instrument Position	☐	☐	☐	☐

Musical Criteria:				
Rhythm	☐	☐	☐	☐
Tone Quality	☐	☐	☐	☐
Accuracy of Notes	☐	☐	☐	☐
Accuracy of Bowing	☐	☐	☐	☐
Intonation	☐	☐	☐	☐
Expression	☐	☐	☐	☐

Figure 4.3. Exemplary Rating Scale—Comprehensive
Individual Student Performance in a String Ensemble—Check-Box Style

Definitions of Rating Scale Points for Student Performance Rating Sheet

- Right Hand Position

  1. Student does not demonstrate correct placement of fingers or functional bow hold.
  2. Student demonstrates some correct finger placement, but not all aspects are correct.
  3. Student has correct finger placement, but does not demonstrate functional bow hold or fluidity.
  4. Student demonstrates consistent finger placement and functional bow hold.

- Left Hand Position

  1. Left hand and arm is completely incorrect.
  2. Left arm is in correct position but wrist/hand do not address instrument correctly.
  3. Left arm, wrist, and hand are in correct position, but are not flexible.
  4. Left arm is fully functional.

- Posture/Instrument Position

  1. Posture is not lengthened or balanced.
  2. Posture is lengthened and balanced, but instrument is not held correctly.
  3. Posture and instrument position are basically correct but student does not display mobility/functionality.
  4. Posture and instrument position are consistently correct and functional.

- Rhythm

  1. Student does not keep a steady beat.
  2. Student keeps a steady beat but does not display a sense of meter.
  3. Student keeps steady beat and displays sense of meter.
  4. Student plays both macrobeats and microbeats with precision.

- Tone Quality

  1. Tone quality is unfocused, surface sound, or inconsistent.
  2. Student produces correct basic tone.
  3. Tone quality is consistent, and student is able to control tone using bow placement, speed, or weight.

4. Tone quality is full and consistent, and colors are controlled. Vibrato is used.

- Accuracy of Notes

  1. Multiple errors are present; student is unable to play notes correctly; may indicate lack of preparation or material that is too difficult.
  2. Student performs with control, although some errors are present.
  3. Student performs with fluency; errors are infrequent.
  4. Student performs with complete mastery of notes; no errors.

- Accuracy of Bowing

  1. Bowing and articulation markings are not followed.
  2. Student plays with correct bowings.
  3. Student plays with correct bowings and articulations.
  4. Student plays with correct bowings, articulations, and bow distribution.

- Intonation

  1. Intonation is consistently incorrect.
  2. Student has general sense of intonation, but is inconsistent in finger placement.
  3. Finger placement is consistent and basic intonation is accurate.
  4. Student adjusts intonation for color and tonality.

- Expression

  1. Student plays without expression or phrasing.
  2. Basic elements of phrasing are correct.
  3. Student plays with correct phrasing and style.
  4. Student plays with correct phrasing, style, and articulation.

Tenure . . .
does *not* protect an incompetent teacher.
It exposes an inadequate system of evaluation.
If there is no adequate system of assessing student achievement,
there will be no means of providing adequate assessment of teacher
competence, as a means of either providing professional growth or dismissal.

MUSIC AND THE BRAIN: UNDERSTANDING THE RESEARCH IS KEY TO ITS PROPER USE

Contributed by Stephen Benham, Ph.D.

Budget deficits are the most frequent reason we encounter for the elimination of music programs. However, as you've read elsewhere in this book, financial problems simply reveal the underlying philosophies and priorities that are already held by the decision makers. *The number-one goal of the music educator, then, should be to build a program that serves a large portion of the school population and where student achievement is high, teaching is based on sound educational practice, the program is relevant to the community, and drop-out rates are low.* The students in the program, through demonstrated success, are then the best advocates for the program. Parents will not permit a program to be dropped when they see their students achieving at a high level.

Unfortunately, as we've seen, cuts can come even in the most ideal situations. It's at this point that the music educator often begins the search for anything that will demonstrate music's importance in the overall education of the child. Because the rush for advocacy materials is typically reactive, teachers don't always have the time to adequately review research and have to rely on the work other individuals, associations, and agencies.

It is at this point that music educators face their greatest challenge. As you've likely noticed, much of current advocacy efforts focuses on research related to the extramusical benefits of music education, specifically, improvement on intelligence tests, math and reading scores, spatial reasoning tests, and so on. This is a result of the overall emphasis within the educational establishment on federal and state funding related to student achievement in those areas. It's not surprising that advocates seek to use research on music education and these other subject areas as an opening for advocacy efforts. However, many teachers inherently balk at this approach, as it diminishes the larger value and role of music education for their students.

My goal in this section isn't to revisit the need for responsible advocacy. Instead, my purpose here is to provide the music educator with an understanding of how to appropriately and effectively use music education research in advocacy efforts. As advocates, we need to use every tool at our disposal to defend our programs. However, arguments that convince one group of the value of music may not affect another group. This is why our advocacy arsenal must include valid research that speaks to many different perspectives, including financial, philosophical, and psychological.

The information presented here will help you correctly identify and interpret research studies about music and academic achievement. You'll also see how to avoid common pitfalls that inadvertently weaken your case, such as overstating or inaccurately presenting research results, incorrectly using research language, or inadvertently misrepresenting research findings.

Research, Public Opinion, and Policy

In case you hadn't noticed, we are bombarded on a perpetual basis by research—polls about politics, new findings in the field of medicine, and business trends, for example, seem to make their way into daily news reports. And there's a good reason for this: It's part of how the American people think and process information. Most of us are well aware of how frequently—and often successfully—advertisers, market researchers, and public relations firms use research to sell products.

Research isn't only a tool for marketing, though. It's a device used by the media, politicians, and special interest groups in an attempt to sway public opinion. Research results (typically those that are favorable to a specific individual or group) are used to promote personal agendas, advocate for social change, or push for reform (educational, social, political, etc.).

Educational reformers are especially fond of using research. For example, research on the needs of adolescent youth was a primary reason for the push to shift from junior high schools to middle schools in the 1990s. During the 1980s, the release of the *Nation at Risk* report led to calls for increased attention on "the basics" of education (math, science, and reading). More recently, low achievement in some sectors of the public school system in the United States, as revealed by the research of the *National Assessment of Educational Progress* (http://nces.ed.gov/nationsreportcard/), commonly referred to as the NAEP, led to the implementation of the federal No Child Left Behind Act (NCLB) of 2001 (www.ed.gov/nclb/landing.jhtml). The results of NCLB are felt daily in every classroom of every public school across the country. By the way, if you haven't read the response to the effects of NCLB on the teaching of liberal arts in America's public schools, be sure to check out the following report released in March 2004 by the Council for Basic Education: *Academic Atrophy: The Condition of the Liberal Arts in America's Public Schools.*

Music education advocates are relative newcomers to evaluating the merits of research studies and then using the results to advance the case for a complete music education for every child. In the late 1970s and early 1980s, the beginnings of the music education advocacy movement (sparked by budget recessions, property tax relief, etc.) helped push interest in music education research outside the university. Advocates began to understand that research might be an effective means to sustain endangered music education programs.

Understanding Research Language

One of the problems for all consumers in understanding research is that the terminology can be confusing. Researchers have their own language and use common words in a slightly different way. While this might seem like a conspiracy on the part of researchers, it's actually a good thing. If research is to be useful, the words used to describe research have to be always defined and used consistently. This means we have to understand what the words mean and how they are used in a research setting. The terminology guide below will help you in understanding research studies, and more importantly, recognize spurious research when it comes your way!

A word of caution: In order to protect the public and uphold professional ethics and standards, most fields of research have extremely strict procedures for reviewing and publishing research results. There are hundreds of journals devoted to research in various fields (such as the *Journal of Research in Music Education*), and these journals generally have boards of review that maintain strict control over research publications. With this in mind, the consumer needs to be wary of self-reported research or research that comes from non-refereed journals, as this research may not meet professional standards. I listed a few key terms below to assist you in identifying and clarifying some of the issues.

- *Prove*: In spite of the number of times that we hear that new research *proves* something, researchers generally frown on the use of the word "prove." Why? Research results are reported according to a scale of probability or confidence, which is calculated using a variety of statistical tools. It's not really possible to calculate research results exactly (you generally can't survey every person from a certain population of people; you have to be selective). Instead researchers use statistical measurements to estimate and determine the validity and reliability (see below) of their research. So researchers tend to avoid words that indicate absolutes. Instead of *prove*, researchers will use words like *demonstrate* or *support*.
- *Accuracy*: Accuracy means that the results were calculated correctly and that the researchers didn't make any mistakes in the mathematics of the report.
- *Validity*: If research is valid, it means that the researchers actually measured what they intended to measure. Why is this important? From time to time, researchers may make incorrect claims (either intentionally or unintentionally) about certain aspects of their research. There are statistical formulas for determining if research meets the minimum standards of validity.
- *Reliability*: This means that the results are consistent and repeatable. If we conducted the same research again, we'd get the same results. As

with validity, there are statistical formulas and minimum standards for research to be considered reliable.

- *Correlation* and *causation*: The difference between these two terms is very important and often misunderstood. If research results demonstrate a high correlation between two events, it doesn't necessarily mean that one item is affecting the other. It just means that there is some type of relationship between the two. Additional tests must be conducted to determine what type of relationship there is, or whether there is a cause-and-effect relationship (causation). So, to use a common phrase, correlation doesn't mean that there is causation.

- *Significant*: In research terminology, the term *significant* has to do with statistical measurements, rather than practical importance. Research findings that are considered to be reliable usually need to demonstrate statistical significance of .01 or better, which means that the results of the research will be true in 99 out of 100 cases.

- *Substantial*: In research terminology, the term *substantial* has to do with the size of the effect. Like the word *significant* above, research use of the word *substantial* differs from the everyday use of the word. In the mind of a layperson, there may be a substantial body of research, but this doesn't necessarily relate to whether or not the size of the effect was substantial.

- *Generalizability*: Can the results of the research be applied to other people or populations? For example, do things that cause disease in mice also cause disease in people? Sometimes, but not always. Researchers are typically interested in the question of generalizability because the results of the research then may have greater meaning for more people.

How to Interpret Research: Know Your Terminology

At the height of budget cutbacks in the 1980s and 1990s, music education advocates were hungry for any type of research that might bolster their case in the court of educational public opinion (also known as school boards and administrations). Because the field of music education research was still relatively new, and so little was known about music education and child development, advocates tended to grasp onto *any* research that said something positive about music education—even if the research wasn't intended to be used this way. The most popular claims have had to do with research that demonstrates a positive correlation (see above) between music education and improvements in other cognitive areas, like reading, mathematics, spatial reasoning, and so on. While our profession intuitively likes the thought that music education is so wide reaching, we've gotten into some trouble because we have frequently misused the research reports or overstated our case. Let me explain.

When we hear that a research report claims that some type of music instruction has positive effects on other types of intelligence, we need to first look very closely at the research itself. You'll often find that the researchers haven't actually made those claims. Rather, the research discusses that "music listening," "keyboard training," or some other form of activity has a positive effect on retention, spatial skills, or improved scores on certain intelligence tests. However, is "music listening" or "keyboard training" *really* music education? Some might argue so in the first case, because listening to music is generally part of a music education. But does making music actually have the same effect? Likewise, does keyboard training really train the part of the brain responsible for physical (kinesthetic) intelligence or the part of the brain responsible for musical intelligence? It depends on what's included with the keyboard training. In any case, we need to look very closely at the research itself to determine what the authors are actually stating.

A frequent claim about music education is that children who study music do better on standardized testing. Again, this type of research demonstrates high correlation, but not necessarily causation. When this is pointed out, advocates frequently bolster their claim by stating that other research shows that students who study music longer demonstrate even higher scores. Unfortunately, none of these arguments rule out other possibilities not included in the research reports. For example, are students who take music already better students? Do they participate in music because they like having a diverse set of experiences? Do students who stay in music longer already have better personal skills that will make them better students? What is the role of the parent or family in helping students to improve? Is it the actual music-making that makes the difference or is it other nonmusical factors, such as participation in group activities, personal accountability, or parental support, that make the difference?

As you can see, the danger in using research to bolster our advocacy cause is filled with potential problems. Antagonistic administrators, school board members, teachers, parents, and members of the community may quickly find holes in our claims if we have overstated, overgeneralized, or misinterpreted research results.

Unfortunately, as I believe has happened in general, we have actually weakened our case for music education, because we seek only to justify music for its nonmusical and/or correlative benefits. For example, in a program in upstate New York, a principal wanted to develop a beginning string program in his elementary school because he felt it would help students improve on standardized reading test scores. When the positive results didn't happen, his support for the music program diminished.

How to Interpret Research Correctly: Ask the Right Questions

When media reports claim music instruction has positive effects on other types of intelligence, you may find that those evaluating the research haven't paid close attention to the details of the study.

Problems occur when individuals confuse activities directly related to musical intelligence with those related to other types of intelligence. For example, keyboard training affects the part of the brain responsible for physical (kinesthetic) intelligence, not the part of the brain responsible for musical intelligence. While spatial and kinesthetic intelligence are both necessary to perform music well, they are very different from activities directly related to musical intelligence such as singing melodies, composing, and so on.

As you select research, ask the following questions:

- Does this study investigate a musical task or a music-*related* task, such as keyboard training (more closely related to spatial intelligence)? In one study, keyboard training improved students' abilities in mathematic reasoning; however, those students who received singing instruction (a musical task) showed *no* improvement in mathematical reasoning.
- Does this study relate to activities offered in your district's classrooms? If you cite a study focused on a task that your students don't do, you may be asked to add that activity to your curriculum and sacrifice other more important items.
- What population was studied? If researchers studied a small group of preschool students, you cannot necessarily draw comparisons to a high school classroom.
- What was the size of the group studied? This is one of the greatest problems in selecting research. Very often, group size is extremely small, meaning research results may not be valid and generalizable. Look closely at what the report says about the validity of the study.

You can see why it's important to look closely at the research to determine what findings researchers are reporting, and then utilize those findings on their own merits.

A Strong Enough Case for Music Education?

When making statements about connections between academic achievement and music, consider other possibilities for success related to music study perhaps not included in the research reports. For example, are students who take music already better students? Do they participate in music because they like having a diverse set of experiences? Do students who stay in music longer possess better personal skills that make them better students? Does music making make the difference or is it participation in group activities, personal accountability, or parental support?

Can you see how we actually weaken our case for music education when we seek only to justify music for its nonmusical and/or ancillary benefits? Say a principal develops an elementary school string program expecting it to help improve standardized reading test scores. When scores don't improve, his support for the music program may diminish, despite strong enrollment, good performance results, and positive community engagement. He may even say music education is taking kids out of reading classes and lowering reading test scores. Bottom line? He's worried his school will be penalized if reading scores do not improve dramatically.

We Can Make Our Case—But We Have to Work Harder at It

Nearly thirty years ago, Howard Gardner, from Harvard University, claimed music is a unique intelligence and cognitive process. Rather than spending so much energy arguing that music helps other academic subjects, I believe we should devote more time to demonstrating that music is a unique way of experiencing the world, a unique aspect of the human existence and a unique mode of self-expression. Further, understanding that music *is* a distinct cognitive process, we should focus on continuing to improve the musical experience for our students—an experience that is comprehensive and should include performing, improvising, and composing/arranging. If our programs provide an outstanding musical experience that is broad-based, relevant, and inclusive, we become proactive in our advocacy rather than reactive. A successful music program serving large numbers of students is the best defense possible.

Let the following ideas guide your development of research-based advocacy arguments:

- Explore resources and websites of affiliate organizations and other professional associations. Be sure your sources are reliable, use them wisely, and beware of hype that often accompanies new research findings.
- Do not overstate, misinterpret, or generalize results to create desirable advocacy messages. Correlative research is fine to use, but be cautious about implying causal links.
- Use research demonstrating that music is a unique form of intelligence. (See Howard Gardner.)
- Use research demonstrating that musical intelligence is crucial to success in global society. (See Eric Jensen and MENC's publication *National Standards for Arts Education*.)

- Use research supporting the view that *all* people have some aptitude in music. By not offering strong music education programs, we *are not educating the whole person* and we are neglecting individuals who demonstrate specific giftedness. (See Sandra Trehub and Edwin Gordon.)
- Use research demonstrating the unique periods of cognitive and emotional development related to music. (See Sandra Trehub and Mary Hager, and Steven Pinker.)
- Use research focusing on the biological basis of music education, especially emotional intelligence, a tool considered critical by many business leaders.
- Contact your local university's music education department. If faculty members are involved in music education research or teaching classes on music education psychology, they may have the most current information.

Conclusion: Reclaiming Advocacy

Research is a useful tool, but it should not be the centerpiece of our advocacy efforts. When using research, distinguish between music's intrinsic and its extra-musical benefits. Both are important, but we have been overly focused on the second category.

Effective advocates proactively use research to develop and enhance music programs, to argue for increased staffing and resources, to improve teaching, and to implement new methods and necessary curricular change. Used properly, quality research can help us to attain our broader goals of reaching a larger number of students, reducing dropout rates, and providing comprehensive and relevant musical experience for our students.

THE MUSIC ADMINISTRATOR

When school music programs face cuts or financial crisis, the music administrator is often the first position to be eliminated. Never heard of this position? It may have already been eliminated, with overall responsibility for the music curriculum now loosely spread among a number of music faculty members. Survival of the music curriculum may then depend solely on the public relations skill of each individual teacher or the voice of the public.

When no music administrator is in charge of the music curriculum, music programs are often poorly administered or weakened. The program may even be reduced to an extracurricular activity, as in districts where the athletic director is appointed "activities" director; suddenly the music department becomes a function that is exclusively extracurricular in nature.

Levels of Music Leadership

Who are (or were) these music leaders? Historically, music administrators were experienced music teachers with great passion for music education. They sought positions of leadership as advocates of music for all children.

However, in many cases they lacked the administrative background or training to fully understand how the system worked. As they assumed their positions, many became painfully aware that they had really been hired by the administration to endorse whatever decisions were passed down to them.

And, to make matters worse, they were given different titles relative to the level of authority of their positions and they worked without specific job descriptions or responsibilities.

Here are a few typical position titles and brief descriptions of duties, listed in descending level of authority. Normally, as the level of authority diminishes, so does the amount of FTE assigned to the position.

- *Director of fine arts*: The director of fine arts position includes supervision of all areas of the arts (usually music, drama, dance, and the visual arts). The term *director* implies an administrative-level position, with authority equivalent to other personnel with a similar title such as the directors of personnel, curriculum, and so forth. In the administrative flow chart, this individual might be responsible to an assistant superintendent.
- *Director of music*: This position is similar to that of the director of fine arts but limited to the music program. This position may be equivalent to or under the supervision of the director of fine arts, depending on the size of the district. This may also be a position in which the director of curriculum is responsible for supervision of arts areas outside of music. This position should have centralized authority over all aspects of music in the district.
- *Music supervisor*: The position of music supervisor is normally a position with district-wide supervision. Unfortunately this often includes only those teachers that are itinerant (elementary general or instrumental music), leaving any supervision of teachers assigned to a single school (e.g., high school band director, middle school choral director) up to the site administrator (principal). Efforts should be made to at least include the music supervisor as an advisor to the site administrator, particularly in the teacher selection and evaluation process.
- *Music coordinator*: This position is often exactly what the term *coordinator* implies. It usually carries significantly less authority, and often serves only as a means of coordinating areas of the music program in which the teacher is assigned to multiple schools. Often this position

simply becomes a vehicle for dispensing information that has "come down from the top."

(Note: The positions listed above are not usually eligible for tenure, and therefore may become very politicized. Any perception of authority to lead or advocate may be erroneous, and attempts to do so have sometimes led to dismissal. People who assume this position from within the district may have the option to go back into the classroom, depending on their seniority as a teacher.)

- *Department chair of music*: These positions are under the authority of any position(s) above, if they exist. It is probably more normal that they exist as part-time positions within an individual school, or related to specific areas of the curriculum (e.g., chair of instrumental music or of choral music).

As mentioned above, there are many school districts that now exist with no music administrator positions whatsoever. This can lead to competition within areas of the music curriculum and conflict. Deterioration of program quality and levels of student participation are often, if not usually, the result.

Your Music Coalition Can Help Make the Case for a Music Administrator

What can your music coalition do to help protect music leadership in your school district? Use the influence of your administrative liaison committee of the music coalition to:

- Insist on specific assignment of the administrative or supervisory duties to someone at the administrative level, preferably to someone with music skill. (Where the administrator is a nonmusician, I suggest the district purchase Robert Culver's *Master Teacher Profile*, a three-hour-and-thirty-two-minute video available at www.reallygoodmusic.com/rgm.jsp?page=cdsvideosdetail&iid=123665.)
- Insist on qualified (by education and experience) music supervisory personnel, with the allocation of FTE appropriate to the size of the district.
- Hold your school administrators responsible for excellence in student achievement in music.

Listed below is an extensive, though not exhaustive, list of responsibilities that could or should fall under the authority of the music administrator position.

- Centralized supervision of music faculty and staff by musically qualified personnel

o Search, recruitment, and interviewing of new staff in cooperation with principals
o Coordination, assignment, and scheduling of current staff, including itinerant teachers
o Evaluation of staff by professionally trained music personnel: professional growth and/or termination
o Coordination of the mentor program
o Providing for professional growth
o Communication with and between music faculty
o Allocation, coordination, and assignment of qualified substitute teachers
o Music program advocacy
o Providing administrative assistance for teachers, thereby relieving job stress and building morale

• Centralized supervision of curriculum

o Development and implementation
o Maintenance of curricular excellence
o Providing advocacy for equal opportunity in music for all students in all schools
o Oversight of program assessment (student achievement)

• Maintenance of a coordinated district music calendar
• Oversight of district honors music performance programs

o Honors concerts
o Field trips
o Festivals

• Centralized budget development and control (accountability)
• Centralized development, maintenance, and control of music teaching resources

o Audio and visual resources and technology
o Miscellaneous teaching materials
o Central music library

• Coordinated and informed purchase, control, and assignment of music and music instruments

o Inventory control
o Assignment to schools

- o Preventive maintenance and repair
- o Piano tuning and repair

- Music leadership for community relations

  - o Parent/teacher communications
  - o Public relations
  - o Annual reports to the administration and board on the state of the music program, its financial viability, and profiles of student participation (recruitment, enrollment, retention, attrition)
  - o Documentation of religious music in the school music program
  - o Multicultural issues in music

If you don't have a centralized position or individual assigned to these tasks, many of these duties are probably not being done. But you cannot ensure any kind of consistent quality experience in music for your children without someone—the music administrator in your district—being charged with the official responsibility for these issues and tasks.

THE MUSIC EDUCATOR AS ADVOCATE

The "Unprofessional"

So often as an educator and a member of the school board I have heard the phrase "I am a professional" from those in the teaching profession. Why? I never hear my physician or lawyer make such statements! It always seemed like a statement made from a defensive position. Was it perhaps that what we did or did not do, or how we acted, prevented us from being perceived that way? What does it mean to be a "professional" music educator?

As I have stated on other occasions, the mission of education is not teaching or educating children. The mission of education is students learning. In the same way that school boards and administrators can make decisions that seem to be adult-(self-)centered instead of student-centered, we are capable of doing the same thing as music educators. The following examples are not examples of a professional music educator. They are taken from actual case studies in which I have served as a consultant.

Example #1: Divide and Conquer

The school district is in a financial crisis. Something must be cut. The principal comes into the band room to meet with the director, and the conversation goes something like this.

Principal: We need to talk. You know we are in financial trouble, and I have to cut something out of music [note the philosophical assumption]. I want to do as little damage to your program as possible, so what can I cut that will do the least damage?

Band Director: I don't have anything to cut. I was going to ask for some additional help. I'm way overloaded!

Principal: Well, here's the way it is. Either you tell me what to cut, or I'll have to make the decision and you will just have to accept it.

Band Director: [in a moderate state of panic] Well, if you have to cut something you should probably cut show choir first. It is the least important thing in our department.

Principal: Well, let's hope we don't have to cut anything, but thanks for the help.

You know where the principal goes next. Right—to the choir room, and the conversation goes something like this!

Principal: We need to talk. You know we are in financial trouble, and I have to cut something out of music [note the philosophical assumption]. I want to do as little damage to your program as possible, so what can I cut that will do the least damage?

Choir Director: I don't have anything to cut. I was going to ask for some additional help. I'm way overloaded!

Principal: The band director said that show choir was the least important thing, and I should cut that first.

Choir Director: Really! Well, if you want to cut something that is unimportant, cut the jazz band. That's a complete waste of time and money.

Principal: Well, let's hope we don't have to cut anything, but thanks for the help.

The principal has accomplished at least two things. The band and choir director are now enemies, and *they* have suggested the cuts. The principal can tell the central administration, the board, and the public that the teachers were a part of the discussion and made these recommendations. (Note: You will notice that the string teacher was left out of this process. That is because the string teacher was most likely off campus teaching at another school during that time. Of course, the principal knows that if the band and choir teacher are divided against each other, they will certainly not support saving a part-time string position in their school.)

Example #2: They're Getting All the Best Students

Recently I was asked to come and assist a group of string parents in getting the string program reinstated into the school district. Although the district music program had received state recognition as music department of the year, the program had been eliminated a year earlier because of a financial crisis. The administration granted permission for my participation in the process (and subsequently asked me to come back and meet with the superintendent and parents in an attempt to resolve the situation with the hope to restore the program).

After a meeting with the parents, it became obvious what had happened. Several parents who had children in both band and orchestra came to me individually and informed me that the band director had told them that the orchestra was "getting all the best students," and that the orchestra program was a detriment to the overall success of the band. They needed to have these students marching.

Then I met with the music teachers, specifically those that were left to teach band, choir, and general music. Here is a summary of what the band directors said.

"What right did you have to come into the school district?"
"We don't want the string program. It takes all the best students."
"Now that the string program is gone, we teach the [middle school] general music classes and use them for band sectional rehearsals."

In other words, it was the band directors who had suggested the elimination of the string program so that there was less competition for students. Unfortunately, this was not a unique experience!

Example #3: We're Going to Double the Amount of Time for Music!

The school district is in financial crisis. Something has to go. The administrative proposal is to eliminate the grades 5 and 6 instrumental music program. The result will be positive, because the administration has said they will double the amount of time for music in the elementary grades. You have to ask: "How are they going to double the time for music if they are eliminating all these music teachers?"

Several years earlier the district superintendent had decided to develop an innovative elementary science program. The district hired one or two specialists to facilitate the program. It was a miserable failure, but the teacher was on tenure now and it seemed as though there was no way to deal with the situation (see section on assessment earlier in the chapter). Here is the plan they developed.

- Eliminate the science specialist positions and curriculum.
- Eliminate the instrumental music program in grades 5 and 6.
- Double the amount of time given to elementary general music so that the classroom teachers could maintain their prep time (another adult-centered decision).

- Use the grades 5 and 6 instrumental music teachers to teach the extra general music time slots.

Here is the solution that the parents, instrumental teachers, and administration developed. Accept the plan with the following condition: The general music curriculum would be revised to incorporate a band, choir, and/or orchestra requirement for all students in grades 5 and 6. Everybody wins, particularly the students!

Unfortunately, there was one elementary general music teacher (who had refused to attend any of the meetings) who had been in the district twenty years. She convinced all the other elementary general music teachers that this would require them to revise their lesson plans and perhaps have larger classes. Although this had all been considered and approved by the other general music teachers, this teacher so divided the ranks that the administration decided to just go ahead and cut the instrumental program to stop the fighting.

As one of my former mentors used to say, "There are some teachers who teach twenty years, and others who teach the same year twenty times!" This was certainly one of the latter. (I should also note that several years later the administration realized the mistake and reinstated the instrumental program. However, that didn't provide an option for all of those students who were denied the opportunity.)

> The greatest detriment to the advancement of music education is often the disunity of our own profession!

Example #4: Heritage or Inheritance

I was called in to help with an elementary instrumental music program that was being cut. I met with all the music teachers. It was an outstanding staff and an outstanding program. The average teacher had been in the district for nineteen years. Every area of the curriculum conveyed nothing but excellence: band, choir, orchestra, and general music. They were the best, and every district around them knew it; but they were being cut. I asked them about their superintendent. The list of offences was unbelievable. I had never heard of any group being treated so badly by an administrator. "How long has he been here?" I asked. It was his first year! They had never met with him to explain their program and who they were—but "all administrators were like that," they said.

The next day I met with the parents. They asked me if I would be willing to meet with the superintendent. So we went together. I asked the superintendent to tell me about the music teachers. The list of offences was long, longer than the teachers' list. I asked him if he had ever met with them.

"No," he said, "I've only been here one year; but I've been an administrator for many years, and all music teachers are like that."

As music educators we have a wonderful heritage. We work hard. We love our art and we strive to pass that on to our students. It is our heritage. Unfortunately, we also inherit the (good and bad) reputation of our predecessors—and those who follow us inherit ours!

> Some of our students will become school board members,
> administrators, or even government leaders.
>
> * * *
>
> How will their experiences impact their decisions about music education?

The "Professional"

What does it mean to be a professional music educator? Among the many possibilities, the professional music educator exhibits the following characteristics.

- Our priorities are music first, the student second, and the job last.
- We support the making of music for all students.
- We value learning above teaching.
- We make clear distinctions between music as a curricular, cocurricular, and extracurricular entity.
- We have high academic and performance standards that are written, specific, achievable, and measurable and have a system of assessment in place that clearly demonstrates individual student achievement.
- We view music as an integrated curriculum, with the various components including general music, choir, band, and orchestra.
- We see our primary goal as developing lifelong makers and patrons of music.

> To be the *best advocate*—be the *best teacher*.

Three case studies provide exemplary models of unity and collaboration. In each example, the music educator was key to preserving the integrity of music within the district.

Example #1: Collaboration, Not Competition

One of my early mentors provided an early illustration of the importance of collaboration in the high school and district where I did my student teaching. All of the music teachers developed a policy to avoid any appearance of competition for students between band, choir, and orchestra. If a student wanted to drop one aspect of the music program for another (e.g., drop band to take choir) they had to complete the following process:

- Write an essay on why the change was important to them.
- Include a description of any issues that led to the change, including possible conflicts with other students or the teacher.
- Submit the written essay to all members of the music department.
- Present an oral summary of the report to the members of the music faculty.

During the oral presentation the music faculty would ask questions of the student as appropriate. Following this the faculty met together to determine whether or not the student's request was legitimate and then submit their approval or disapproval (with reasons for their decision). There were other benefits to this process.

- Students learned to deal with issues in ways other than running from them.
- Students were given responsibilities for making mature decisions.
- Students learned a process of resolving potential conflicts.
- Students learned the importance of unity in managing any organization.

Example #2: It's Time to Get Organized

It was a large district with approximately 100 music teachers. A small group of music teachers decided that it was time to do something about improving the music program in the district. They asked me to come and facilitate a series of strategic planning meetings. At the beginning of my first presentation someone from the back of the auditorium shouted, "Stop!" You could have heard a pin drop. Then he declared, "We're being asked to come here and work together to build this program. We haven't had a meeting in at least ten years. Can we just take some time to get to know each other before we start? I don't even know who the people are that teach in my own area."

We took a break. People just introduced themselves and talked for a while. It was the start of an extended time period in which the entire community began to come together. Leadership emerged, and the district now has made significant strides in bringing back its music program.

Example #3: United We Stand

Early in the fall the district began discussing the impending budget crisis and probable elimination of the elementary instrumental music program.

For over a decade the instrumental music teachers had been meeting together after school once a month. It was primarily an informal time, but also one in which they discussed any issues they were having as individual teachers or departments.

As a result of these regular meetings they were already well organized when they received the word of the administrative proposal to make the cuts. They had a telephone bank (before the emergence of e-mail groups) in which they only needed to make one call to activate the music coalition. Emergency meetings were called and the process of advocacy was set up three months before the public announcement of the administrative proposal.

The teachers and parents came together politically and with the correct information. The school board rejected the proposed cuts, and the program was saved.

BUILDING RELATIONSHIPS: ONE KEY TO SUCCESS

One of the great things I have learned about music teachers is that they tend to be very passionate about their work. They are often teaching before school, after school, during lunch hours, and even during their prep hours. I have heard more than one superintendent say that they wished all their teachers worked as hard as music teachers, and that all teachers cared as much about the individual student as music teachers do.

Our ability to succeed as music educators is often directly related to our ability to establish relationships with the various constituents of the entire community. We need to make sure that we treat all people and the positions they hold with respect.

My first superintendent was a wonderful leader and educator. One day I stormed into his office and vented my frustrations, none of which were with him. (My first teaching job consisted of six bands and four choirs.) He never said a word. I walked out, turned around, and came back into his office to apologize. "I'm sorry," I said. "I was upset." He said in his own gracious way, "I noticed that." We had a good talk, and I vowed never to act that way with him again.

What I have observed in my own teaching and in my consulting efforts is that music educators are not particularly good at advocating for their own issues, at least not in ways that provide for good relationships. Here are some suggestions that may help you avoid some of the pitfalls that we may have inherited from some of our predecessors, and some of which we may have affirmed.

- The student is first.
- Develop a community music coalition. Let your music coalition represent the program to your administration and at board meetings—avoid

the appearance of being in conflict of interest or insubordinate. They have the power. You don't.

- Remember that you are an employee of the community who serves under the board and administration. Never attack individuals or their positions.
- Work collaboratively with other music teachers in support of music education.
- Remember that nonmusic teachers have some of the same frustrations you do. You can't just come and demand the students because of your schedule. Work with them to resolve any issues. If they get involved in the process, they will be more apt to support the decision.
- Don't handle any money. You put yourself in a position of false accusation.
- Don't have an office without a window. You put yourself and the students in a position of potential compromise or false accusation.
- Don't get into an athletics-versus-music battle. You will identify yourself as extracurricular. Your students and parents are most likely involved in and supporting both. Furthermore, you will lose before the public.

If you have to tell people that you are a professional, are you acting like one? If you are acting like a professional, will you have to tell anyone?

II

THE PROCESS OF
MUSIC ADVOCACY

5

Understanding the Process

THE POLITICS OF PROCESS

It is mid-January. My telephone rings and I hear the stressed voice of a parent, a local music retailer, or a music teacher about to lose a job. "I just learned that our school district's administration is proposing to eliminate the elementary instrumental music program. The school board votes next week. What can I do?"

This all-too-common scenario shows why all music advocates need to know everything they can about how and when decisions are made in their school district. Understanding this decision-making process depends upon two main things: the timeline involved and the roles of the key decision makers.

DECISION DRIVERS

Let us all recognize that federal and state legislative bodies that often have very little understanding of the educational process impact much of what occurs in a school district. Consequently, a district can often become paralyzed in its decision-making process. Two typical examples demonstrate this effect.

1. Depending on the political climate and status of legislative actions for education, a district may need to formulate several budget options in order to be prepared for increasing or decreasing per-pupil financial allocations.

2. Unreasonable or unrealistic expectations may be placed on a district. Typical examples include demands for increasing test scores, graduation rates, or other reform issues. These may come in the form of mandates without funding.

It is also important to recognize the distinction between decision makers and decision drivers. The decision makers will nearly always take their cues from the decision drivers. The primary pressure on when to make decisions comes from a variety of adult-centered issues. In order to successfully function within your school system you will need to determine several factors.

- What is the normal practice and timeline for making decisions in your district—who or what body is the primary decision maker, and where do they get their information?
- How does that compare with what the law says about the public right and responsibility to determine school district policy?
- What or who are the decision drivers in your district?

TIMING IS (ALMOST) EVERYTHING

The timeline is usually driven by the academic year. At the start of every school year, the administration and board establish goals and objectives for the year and prioritize items for discussion.

By law, all school board meetings are open to the public, except where local law allows them to be closed (such as on personnel issues). Board agendas are available as public information, but not necessarily widely publicized or read. On numerous occasions, school boards and administrations appear to have adopted a policy of minimal publicity, thereby insulating, isolating, or even excluding the public from input into the decision-making process. This may be particularly true in an environment of financial crisis, boundary changes, or educational reform. The apparent underlying motivation seems to be that if the public becomes involved it will only complicate the decision-making process. Since it is normal that few people attend school board meetings, the impending crisis often comes as a complete surprise to the community.

INFORMATION IS POWER

So, the first thing successful music advocates need to do is *attend school board meetings*. This is one of the very best ways to learn about any impending crisis or issues that may affect the music curriculum. It also puts you in the same room with most of the key players in your district; as with anything else in life, it is helpful to get to know and develop some relationships with these people *before* there's a major problem. And, as a very important byproduct, you'll begin to understand how the process works in case you need to use it.

By October or November—several weeks into the school calendar—administrative decisions about programs to cut have already been determined. However, the final and official board vote on proposed cuts is not made until the district gauges public reaction. Public hearings may be held at this time to provide a better sense of public opinion. If people fail to show up or express their opinions, this may be interpreted as permission or a mandate to make the proposed cuts.

The first public awareness of any issues often comes in January, roughly five months into the school year. This is when the administration prepares to register secondary students for the next academic year. Site administrators need to know how many teaching positions are available to calculate course offerings, class sizes, and positions to eliminate. If budget cuts or educational reforms are being proposed, those decisions must be made before registration materials are completed.

The next major event in the decision-making process is notifying teachers about the loss of their jobs. The legal deadline for this is normally between March 1 and April 15. These "pink slip" letters may give you a more accurate picture of the proposed cut list, including so-called hidden cuts.

The final decision regarding staffing or other changes related to budget or reform is not normally made until the board's last meeting before the end of the fiscal year. In most cases, adoption of the final budget must be made by the last meeting in June. It's important to remember that changes—both positive and negative—may be made up to and at this time.

IT'S NOT OVER 'TIL THE AUDITOR SINGS

In cases where music program reductions are already in place, don't give up hope! It may still be possible to override cuts and reinstate programs or teaching positions. This is because final audits for the previous school year are not completed when cuts are made. If final audits indicate a greater fund balance than anticipated, you may still be able to convince your district to reinstate lost music positions.

PAY SPECIAL ATTENTION TO REFERENDUMS

Referendums to increase school district funding (both bond and levy) are another driving force in the decision-making timeline. Referendums may be placed before voters at any time; some are up to the district, others governed by state law. The decision to hold a public referendum may somewhat alter the above sequence of events; however, your administration and board will continue to maintain the basic outline of their decision-making process even while preparing for both the success and failure of any referendum. A list of proposed cuts related to the potential failure of a referendum is often developed. While such cut lists may provide some degree of financial reality, cuts are often developed to give voters opposed to the cuts an incentive to go to the polls.

In my opinion, this is a dangerous strategy, especially if the referendum fails. The vote may be interpreted as a public mandate to cut any programs on the list. Therefore, it is of utmost importance to keep any potential music cuts off that list!

THE POWER OF PROACTIVE INVOLVEMENT

Active involvement in the process by the administrative liaison committee of your local music coalition will prevent the "surprise" announcement of proposed cuts to music that are so typical in a financial crisis. A proactive music coalition is far more effective than one operating from a reactive or defensive position.

Knowledge *is* power, and a proactive, well-informed, and visible music coalition definitely has the power to prevent music programs from being cut. In one district where I worked, a local music coalition was formed after the community came together to defeat proposed cuts to their music program. This music coalition was such a positive community force that the administration added a new step to their decision-making process: any proposed changes were submitted to the music coalition *before* being placed on any official agenda. Now *that's* noteworthy progress!

PUBLIC OPINION SURVEYS

When facing any difficult financial crisis, school board members and administrators may feel a survey is a good measure of community opinion about educational values. They think that using surveys is a good way to inform people about the seriousness of the situation.

However, since community participation is voluntary—and the validity of results will vary depending on public awareness of the survey, trust in the administration, and the content, design, and delivery of the survey—surveys may, in fact, jeopardize music programs. Here's why, along with some suggestions to help your district avoid falling into the "public survey trap."

Why Do Administrators Use Surveys?

Surveys are used for many reasons, and not all of them are above-board. Besides informing the public about a financial crisis, the possibility of closing or merging schools in the district, or the need to raise taxes, surveys may also be used to:

- establish a basis for a levy referendum to increase school funding;
- inform (or sometimes threaten) the public about probable cuts if school funding is not increased;
- gauge what community members value most and least so cuts will create the least negative reaction.

Surveys are normally distributed to district residents in one or more of the following ways: regular mail (with or without return envelopes); e-mail or downloadable forms (obviously, only to those with Internet access); internal school mail (school employees only); random telephone interviews; and distribution at local PTA or committee meetings, among others.

Do you begin to see how access and convenience plays a major role in validity of results?

Common Survey Pitfalls

Statisticians, marketers, and researchers are well aware of the problems associated with improperly conducted surveys. When surveys are not done properly, results can be skewed, uninformative, invalid, and destructive.

Consider the following dangerous scenarios:

- Intentional and strategic formatting can create a desired (biased) response.
- Poor wording or unclear definitions can create inaccurate results.
- Improperly conducted surveys can reveal the bias or philosophy of the researcher.
- Attitudes of the researcher may also be revealed by omission or by lack of solicitation of broader community input.
- Location of music categories or programs on the survey can reflect administrative philosophy (i.e., music is, or should be, extracurricular).
- Music may be listed as a simple line item title from a budget, perhaps using terms or categories not understood by survey participants.
- Surveys may reveal a lack of knowledge about the financial viability of music as a curricular entity.
- Lack of participation by the community may not be apparent until a complete, impartial analysis of the results is conducted.

The primary danger of poorly designed or improperly conducted surveys, however, is that they may still be interpreted as a public mandate—to make cuts in music programs, for example—even if community participation levels are low. If the necessary funding level is not achieved, or if a levy referendum fails to pass, citing survey results can be extremely dangerous for music and the arts.

One Case Study Illustrates Several Problems with Using Surveys

Background

This district of slightly over 11,000 students was facing an $8 million deficit. If a levy referendum failed to pass, 150 of the 700 teachers would be eliminated. A public opinion survey was sent to 60,000 residences that included all staff and employees. The survey listed 200 programs (nine of which were music) for possible elimination. Respondents were asked to assign the following rankings to each program:

Category A: Programs most important to retain
Category B: Cut these programs first
Category C: Save these programs if you can

Preliminary Results

The voters rejected the levy referendum (probably because the teachers' union was negotiating for a 16 percent pay increase at the same time). The district interpreted the "no" vote as a mandate to make cuts based on survey results. The administration proposed—and the board approved—a 70 percent reduction in orchestra staff and a 48 percent reduction in band staff. Among other negative results, this would have caused the elimination of the entire elementary instrumental curriculum.

The Parents Committee Takes Action

Advocates discovered only 211 surveys (out of 60,000) had been completed and returned to the district. This low response rate rendered survey results invalid and no one in the district bothered to collate actual results. However, the parents did and what they discovered is illustrated in table 5.1.

The Factual Analysis

Those who responded to the survey viewed music as equal in importance to other curricular and cocurricular subjects. Music was outranked only by

Table 5.1 Public Survey Results: Programs Most Important to Retain

Music Programs (9 out of 200 programs listed in survey)	Category Rank as (A) Most Important to Retain (out of 200)	Percentile Rank as (A) Most Important to Retain
Music: Secondary Schools	37	82
Summer School Music	38	81
Music: Elementary	50	75
Music: Cocurricular, JHS	62	69
Music: Cocurricular, SHS	65	68
Elementary Instrumental Music	71	65
Music Curriculum	80	60
Music Instrument repair	88	56
District String Program	110	45

the traditional "three Rs" and federal/state mandated programs. Music actually outranked all (nonmusic) extracurricular activities as "most important to retain." The administration had completely discounted the survey results *except* to use the survey to justify the recommendation they had planned to make throughout the entire process.

I am pleased to tell you that the community music coalition united to confront the district on their faulty interpretation of the survey results and the negative impacts their recommendations would have on the music program and the entire educational system. No components of the music curriculum were eliminated, and all teaching positions in music were retained.

What Should Advocates Do When Facing a Public Survey?

1. Do everything you can to keep the music curriculum off the list of potential or suggested cuts—and make sure music is not listed as cocurricular or extracurricular.
2. Make sure music is not placed in direct competition with or above athletics, for example, giving the possible impression that cuts should be made in music first.
3. If a survey is to be used, make sure it is developed and/or reviewed by an independent researcher or survey expert before distribution and, in the case of telephone surveys, consider using a professional to conduct the interviews.
4. Make sure surveys are widely distributed and available in both downloadable (online) and printed (mailed) formats.

5. Once the survey process is complete, make sure an independent analysis of results is conducted.
6. Publish the results for community information.

CRISIS MANAGEMENT

In any crisis it is important to identify the issues first. These will tend to fall into one or more of the following categories.

- Faculty issues
- Curricular issues
- Student participation issues
- Economic issues

Embedded in each of these issues will be some that are adult-centered and some that are student-centered. It is important to identify and distinguish between the two. As you develop your advocacy plan make sure that your efforts are directed toward the specific issues. For example, in a financial crisis a strong philosophical presentation will not be nearly as effective as demonstrating your financial viability; or, if you are making a budget request for funding, it is important to show the direct impact on the students if your request is denied.

6

How to Develop and Use Impact Statements

One of the greatest and most common mistakes advocates make in attempting to save music programs is suggesting cuts or compromises to preserve preferred parts of a music program. Based on my experience, offering these suggestions is one of the primary reasons that music programs are vulnerable to cuts.

THE NEGATIVE POWER OF SUGGESTION

Here's the basic scenario: Often an administrator who assumes music cuts may be needed will contact a specific teacher, music supervisor, or music booster and pose a question such as, "What cut(s) will do the least damage to the music program?" If anyone suggests a possibility, it will be cut. The administration and board are then cleared of any blame or responsibility, and the public is told cuts were based on suggestions from the music people.

I refer to this administrative strategy as "divide and conquer."

Though saving preferred parts of the music program may be tempting bait, do not fall into this trap! It is the job of the administration and board to balance the budget. It is your responsibility as an advocate to clearly show the negative impacts of any proposed cuts to the music program.

THE VALUE OF IMPACT STATEMENTS

Simply put, impact statements define the short- and long-term results of any administrative proposals to cut music. Some purposes for developing impact statements include the following:

1. To keep the issue of how student opportunities in music may be negatively impacted in front of the administration, the school board, and particularly the public.
2. To demonstrate any incorrect assumptions made by the administration related to music cuts, particularly regarding economic viability.
3. To demonstrate to the public the potential fiscal and curricular misconceptions or problems with the administrative proposal as related to proposed music cuts.

BUILD SUCCESSFUL IMPACT STATEMENTS ON ACCURATE INFORMATION AND RESEARCH

The impact statements you develop will vary, and depend upon the information you extract from documents provided by the administration and board. In developing impact statements it is important to make sure all of your information is accurate! Do not make assumptions, do not guess at statistics, and document everything (time, place, source, etc.). As you're building your case and interpreting the data collected, please refer to other parts of the book for additional examples (case studies, FTE value discussion in chapter 8, etc.).

Usually you will formulate a response that completes a statement. For example, "If the district adopts its proposal to eliminate 4.0 FTE positions in instrumental music, it will have the following impact(s)." Impacts normally fall into one (or more) of four categories. Each is listed below with sample impact statements based on a proposed elimination of 4.0 FTE instrumental music teachers. (Note: These statements are all minimal. You will soon see that additional research must be done to develop strong, relevant, and more complete impact statements for each specific situation.)

Faculty Impacts

- The cuts proposed by the administration will reduce the instrumental music staff by 50 percent.
- The elimination of 50 percent of the instrumental music staff will make it impossible to provide music instruction at all schools in the district. (Specify which schools will lose their programs.)

Curricular Impacts

- Instrumental music will not be offered as an option for students until grade 7.
- Individual and small group lessons will not be staffed.
- All beginners will be placed together in large classes in a single class, regardless of the diversity of instruments and skill levels present.

Student Participation Impacts

- Attrition rates will increase due to lack of satisfactory progress and supervision on student achievement.
- There may be legal challenges from the community related to equal access.
- Based on national case studies, the loss of the elementary instrumental music curriculum will result in a 65 percent reduction of instrumental music students in the higher grades.

Economic Impacts

- The average (secondary) instrumental music teacher carries a student load equivalent to 1.2 classroom teachers.
- The district will need to replace each music teacher eliminated with a minimum of 1.2 classroom teachers unless class sizes are significantly increased.
- In the long term, losing the cost-benefit advantages of large music performance classes (e.g., band) will negate any cost savings anticipated by the district. It will also prevent many students in the district from the possibility of participating in instrumental music.

As you study any proposals made by your administration, you will be able to develop many similar impact statements based upon the uniqueness of your situation. The more effective you are in developing statements that directly relate to the administrative proposals and their negative impact on students and the budget, the more effective you will be in advancing your case.

Remember: A cut is any decision made that will negatively impact the ability of any student to participate in making music.

> Rule #1: No cuts or compromises should be suggested by
> any member of the community, including the music coalition,
> music educators, or the music supervisor!

Normally threats to music programs come in one or more categories, each of which will be discussed in the following chapters:

- Educational reform
- Hidden agendas
- Budget crisis
- Hidden cuts

7

Crisis Management: Educational Reform

AN OVERVIEW AND SOME ADVICE

In my experience as both educator and consultant, I have watched an array of educational reforms come and go—and, in some cases, come and go again. These reforms may seek to make changes in specific curricular areas, such as the now-ancient "modern math" movement, or make changes in the entire structure of the educational institution. Regardless of the type of reform being proposed, or its effects on students, there's only one thing that is true of all of them: *Reform means change. It does not guarantee improvement!*

While student achievement is usually stated as the primary motivation for any educational reforms, there are often secondary motivations related to specific adult issues (such as budgets, staffing, public relations, and keeping teachers or parents happy). For the most part I believe people at all levels want educational improvement, but the motivations are diverse and, frankly, not all positive. I am not suggesting that any or all educational reforms are bad. My intention is to make all of us aware that any environment of change is an opportunity to improve our music programs. And, when any suggestion is made to reform, it's definitely a time to be aware of potential dangers to the music curriculum.

Some Key Points to Consider

Here are some positive action points to help you and your music coalition navigate through the process of change:

- As a music coalition, be involved in school district politics at all levels.
- Be proactive. Make sure that at least one member of your music coalition is on every district task force *and* that at least one member attends every school board meeting.
- Recognize that any discussion of change probably has implications for the music program.
- During any discussions of change, determine the primary motivations as early as possible, then search for possible secondary (adult-centered) motivations.
- Identify the key components of the change(s) under consideration and how those changes might impact the music program from four primary perspectives: faculty and staffing, curriculum (scope and sequence), student participation, and economy (budget).

As you become involved, make every effort to hold all participants to actions or decisions that are student-centered in their outcome. You may even be able to serve as a catalyst for improvements in the music program by becoming involved in the process.

Building Relationships Is the Best First Step

The key to successfully supporting your music program through such times is the development of an attitude of trust with those making the decisions. Trust comes from relationships. Relationships come from time. In other words, the longer you wait to organize your music coalition and mobilize advocates for proactive involvement in the decision-making process in your school district, the more difficult it will be to work for solutions that positively impact your music program.

MIDDLE SCHOOLS OR JUNIOR HIGH SCHOOLS?

For several decades now, I have watched school districts switch from junior high to middle school configurations, and back again, in cyclical patterns that have sometimes led me to question the motivation of the decision-making process. It is not my intent here to evaluate the middle school movement. Rather, I'll reveal some of the secondary motivations for these changes and present the issues that may have positive or negative impact on the ability of all students to make music.

Basically, the middle school movement is concerned with students from ages ten to fifteen who are in various stages of physical, emotional, sociological, and intellectual development that coincide with adolescence. One of the primary motivations for having a middle school is to emphasize a process, a support system, and a curriculum focused on student-centered decision making.

Common themes in the middle school movement include the following:

Teaching Teams

- Teaching teams are developed, usually within the perceived core subjects.
- Teaching teams have a common planning time, often equivalent to two class periods per day. Non-core teachers often teach six (out of seven) classes per day, compared to only five per day for the core subjects.
- The teaching team moves with each student cohort as they progress through the middle schools grades.
- Normally these teaching teams do *not* include the arts.

Environment of Learning

- Students' social skills improve with interaction and long-term support from teaching teams.
- Specialized instruction and certification of teachers provides insight into student behavior, learning styles, and development.
- Reduced class size increases learning and interaction.

Integrated Curricula

- Teachers develop an integrated curriculum for the subjects that are included in the teaching team.
- Common planning is intended to provide for the development of challenging content while providing maximum interest.
- The emphasis is on assessment and advising, not just grading, with the aim of developing students' critical thinking skills.

The Exploratory "Wheel"

- A broad range of subjects is explored in shortened courses.
- Reduced class sizes in exploratory courses may be very expensive.
- This structure enables the hiring of part-time teachers who don't qualify for benefits, a potentially significant cost savings.
- Nonessential (non-core) courses may be moved to the "wheel" or only scheduled on an alternate-day basis (e.g., music may alternate with physical education, or instrumental music may alternate with vocal music).

- Some music teachers have used the "wheel" as a means of facilitating sectional classes for ensembles.

For more information on middle school philosophy, go to the National Middle School Association website at www.nmsa.org.

Secondary Motivations

Despite these intended outcomes, in visiting many school districts over the past years as a music advocate, I've often realized the movement to a middle school grade alignment may have little or nothing to do with these middle school philosophies. Two main issues surface as secondary issues: overcrowding and availability of space, and a financial crisis.

A Solution to Overcrowding

The more significant of these secondary motivations relates to the use of space (facilities, or housing of students) and the distribution of the student population. I have yet to witness a situation in which space usage was not a major player in the process of adopting a middle school concept.

What typically happens is that a school system that is overcrowded in a certain area of the district, or at a certain level of instruction, needs to move students to other schools in the district that have space. To avoid the most volatile of all school issues (boundary changes), the district proposes a change from junior high to middle schools, while adopting few changes in the way it actually delivers education. A good indication of this is the movement of lower grades (5 or 6) into the former junior high school, while maintaining the previous format of instruction for those grades. Little really changes except the lower grades attend classes in a different school building.

Relieving Financial Constraints

A financial crisis, either real or perceived, may accompany this movement of students. The district may make significant changes that are perceived to resolve a financial crisis. This may involve the elimination or reduction of various aspects of the music curriculum. It may also be used as a means of resolving other issues in the district, such as the elimination of elementary "pull-out" instrumental music classes.

Whenever a group of concerned parents of music students contacts me about impending changes, I ask a few basic questions:

- Who is the individual or group leading the reform effort?
- What are the obvious and hidden agendas?

- What are the potential negative effects of the change?
- Is it possible to improve your music program by putting the proposed reform in place?

Agents of Change

I have found that new administrators in a district are leading the motivation behind most efforts at educational reform. Often this appears to be driven by a need to demonstrate leadership as an agent of change. Unfortunately, the elementary instrumental music program is often the first targeted for reduction or elimination.

Table 7.1 summarizes several typical administrative proposals to reduce or eliminate components of the music curriculum that accompany middle school reform. It also details the rationale and hidden motivations for doing so.

The Music Issues

So you're faced with one or more of the proposals shown in the table. What do you do? Here are some interesting facts and ideas you may find useful.

- After more than twenty-five years, our research with national case studies indicates that when a district delays the beginning of instrumental instruction to grade 6, there will be a minimum loss of 65 percent of the enrollment at the middle school level within two years.
- When considering proposed changes, you can try to assess potential impacts on the middle school music curriculum by asking for answers to the following questions:

  o Will the new format allow for curricular diversity (e.g., will there be separate classes for male and female singers as well as mixed choirs)?
  o Will the new format enable placement of students by skill level (e.g., will it enable adequate individualized instruction to meet the needs of gifted or remedial students)?
  o Will the new format provide for small-group homogeneous instruction for beginning, intermediate, and advanced students?
  o If the first year of instruction is delayed until middle school, what measures will be put in place to provide adequate instruction to beginning students? Obviously, the placement of fifty to sixty beginning students playing as many as ten different instruments in a single classroom is far from best practices, and will most certainly increase attrition.

Table 7.1   Administrative Rationale: Middle School Reform and Music Cuts

Proposed Music Cut	Administrative Rationale	Hidden Motivations
Eliminate elementary choral music	• Students can still start in the middle school with minimal effect on learning • Could become part of the general music curriculum	• Perceived cost savings from cut positions • Eliminate complaints about "pull-outs" from elementary classroom teachers • Proposed cuts often come here first, because they will produce the least amount of complaints from parents, especially if placed into the general music curriculum
Eliminate elementary orchestra	• Students can still start in the middle school with minimal effect on learning	• Perceived cost savings from cut positions • Eliminate complaints about "pull-outs" from elementary classroom teachers • Proposed cuts often come here next, because they will produce the least amount of complaints from parents
Eliminate elementary band	• Students can still start in the middle school with minimal effect on learning	• Perceived cost savings from cut positions • Eliminate complaints about "pull-outs" from elementary classroom teachers • Proposed cuts come here next, because they will produce the least amount of complaints from parents
Eliminate elementary general music	• Program is not perceived as curricular, but primarily as a means of providing prep time for classroom teachers	• Perceived cost savings from cut positions • Proposed cuts often come here last because of anticipated protests from classroom teachers • Some districts have eliminated all specialist teachers, moving classroom teacher prep time to the end of the day and sending the students home an hour earlier

Table 7.1 (Continued)

Proposed Music Cut	Administrative Rationale	Hidden Motivations
Reduce middle school general music to six or nine week exploratory "wheel"	• Program is not perceived as curricular, but minimal inclusion may still fulfill state guidelines for music education; further, guidelines are non-binding • Provide exploratory programs to broaden interests for students	• Perceived cost savings from cut positions • "These kids aren't going to be music majors anyway!"
Reduce music performance (band, choir, orchestra) from daily to every-other-day classes	• Program is not perceived as curricular • Music performance is only for the talented few	• Perceived cost savings from cut positions • "These kids aren't going to be music majors anyway!"
Cut middle school lessons and small-group instruction	• Students can learn in the classroom • Parents can provide private lessons for those few students who have exceptional talent • Move lessons to community education	• Perceived cost savings from cut positions • "These kids aren't going to be music majors anyway!"

Note: Our experience indicates that courses in the typical "wheel" tend to be the smallest and, therefore, most expensive.

o Will enough qualified music teachers be available to provide for team instruction in music?

o Will daily rehearsals be facilitated, or will instruction be reduced to every other day? (Tip: One school district has successfully taken advantage of the "wheel" by scheduling individual courses for instruction on homogenous instruments. Students participating in band or orchestra are required to enroll in the "wheel" course that includes their instrument.)

Strong Music Programs in Middle Schools

Here are three other items that will help you maintain the strength of your music program if your district is considering, or has already adopted, the middle school concept:

1. A sequential, written curriculum with specific, achievable, and measurable goals and a system of assessment will provide your district with

relevant data and assist you in demonstrating your music program's viability as a curricular entity. This information will be extremely important to your coalition as advocates try to preserve the integrity of your district's music programming and improve its delivery.

2. Other than a well-organized music coalition, there is probably no greater relationship for you to establish than one with the guidance counselors. Make every effort to demonstrate your credibility as an educator or concerned parent by providing all the guidance counselors in your district with appropriate information on the importance of making music.

3. Remember: *Always* keep the focus on the student—it is their program!

MAGNET SCHOOLS

Simply stated, a magnet school is a school designed to fulfill a perceived special need within a district. Often these schools adopt a structure that emphasizes a particular curricular area, such as (world) language immersion, science, mathematics, and even the arts. Unfortunately, motivation for adopting such programs is often driven by other factors that can negatively impact the opportunity for students to receive equal educational opportunities or a balanced education.

Example #1

The district decides to eliminate the grades 5 and 6 elementary instrumental music program as "too expensive" under the impending financial crisis. On further research the community discovers that there are significant secondary motivations.

- The district also has a language immersion program that has been difficult to schedule, difficult to manage, and has caused significant conflict in the district over issues related to equal access for all students. The publicized financial crisis provides an opportunity to eliminate that program.
- The same financial crisis provided an opportunity to eliminate the grades 5 and 6 elementary instrumental feeder system, a program (incorrectly) perceived as very expensive.

The two issues together had also become a source of irritation to elementary teachers whose classrooms were constantly "interrupted" by the two programs proposed for elimination. Elementary principals saw this as an opportunity to resolve those scheduling issues.

As parents continued their investigation into the situation, a third motivation for eliminating the two programs surfaced. Two elementary principals had traveled to China and returned with plans to develop a program in which twenty-five to thirty elementary Chinese students (at a time) would come to the district to study English and the American system of education. What was the underlying and primary motivation for the two proposed cuts? The only way the program (new teachers, administrators, etc.) could be funded was by eliminating teaching positions in other areas of the curriculum, specifically the language immersion and instrumental music curricula. The music coalition came together, addressed the situation, and worked together with the administration to save the program.

Example #2

A large district (over 34,000 students) was facing two major issues. The first was a financial crisis, and the second the announcement (via the state-publicized "report card") that the district was near the bottom of the scale in student achievement on mandated test scores.

The administrative recommendation was to eliminate all aspects of the music curriculum, except for in one elementary, one middle school, and one high school. This proposal would have eliminated the fine arts coordinator position and reduced the music faculty to approximately 6.0 FTE (see discussion of FTE, FTE value, and SFR in chapter 8) to provide instruction for band, choir, orchestra, and general music. In order to avoid potential lawsuits related to equal access, the administration suggested that this would be a magnet school system for those "few students interested in the arts." In reality, this would have eliminated over 3,000 instrumental and choral students from participation.

These students would have then needed to be placed in regular classrooms with lower numbers of students than in the music performance classes, requiring the addition of more nonmusic teaching positions than were proposed for elimination. The budget crisis would only have exacerbated their financial crisis (see discussion of reverse economics in chapter 8).

In addition, research on statistical data in the district indicated that there was an obvious correlation between lack of student achievement and low funding of the arts. The music coalition was successful in having the program reinstated.

Example #3

A new administrator in the school district wanted to develop a "model" elementary science curriculum, using a magnet school for implementation. Upon development of the curriculum the administration was unable to understand why no one was enrolling for the program. In the superintendent's own words, "I was informed by the parents most interested (in the science magnet) that they would not enroll their students in a school that had no music curriculum. I had to reinstate the music program in order to make the science magnet successful."

Example #4

State funding for education was in an all-time crisis. School districts all over the state were eliminating music programs. The government solution was to provide a state "school of the arts." The money spent on facilities and the organizational structure before the school opened would have enabled building a fine arts center (building) for nearly every school district in the state. In the meantime, thousands of students were denied the opportunity to make music in their own district.

As a friend of mine loves to state, "A magnet school is a program designed to give the elite what they are screaming for, while denying equal access to everyone else." It is not necessarily the concept of magnet programs that is bad. It is the denial of access to all students that is the root of the problem. The development of a magnet school to justify denying access to any curricular area to any individual or group of students is inexcusable, and probably illegal!

For more information, see www.magnet.edu.

CHARTER SCHOOLS

A charter school is simply another form of the magnet school concept. It is a school designed to provide a specialized education for a select group of people. Its primary distinction is the relative degree of independence in its form of governance. These schools can be as unique as the individuals or groups that are organizing them.

From the student (learner) perspective the issue is qualitative. In other words, what standards of assessment have been implemented to measure student achievement and ensure a balanced education?

Another element of significance is where the organization acquires its funding. Is funding of the institution privatized or are funds being extracted from federal, state, or local monies that might otherwise provide an education for the general populace? What regulatory policies have been instituted to provide accountability in management of funds?

These institutions may or may not recognize the importance of including a comprehensive music curriculum for their students.

For more information, see www.uscharterschools.org.

SCHOOL (TAX) VOUCHERS

There is an ongoing public policy debate—acted out in many states in a wide variety of initiatives and regulations—that reflects one fact that cannot be ignored: Tax vouchers ignite strong beliefs and opinions, both for and against, about the use of public money in private and parochial schools.

Tax vouchers have been around since at least the 1980s, and they are a result of a national trend toward freedom of school choice. They are an outgrowth of the open enrollment movement that proposes that the students' family be given the right to choose its own method of educating its children. A secondary motivation of the tax voucher movement is to create a business-like environment that stimulates school improvement through competition to attract students (customers).

How Do Tax Vouchers Work?

The adoption of a tax voucher system is normally the responsibility of a state legislature. Typically the process works like this:

- The legislature determines an annual amount of state funding per child in the public educational system (for example, $7,000).
- The state then determines that a family may receive some form of tax credit for educational expenses for each eligible child (for example, $1,500).
- The family may choose to use this tax voucher as a deduction for educational expenses related to the education of their children and apply it to the cost of sending their children to a private or religious school, or to fund home schooling. The choice to opt out of public schooling is often made because the local public school is perceived to be, and perhaps even may be, academically weak.
- Tax vouchers are primarily intended to assist families who otherwise may not be able to afford to send their children to a school of their choice, for example, a family of low economic means.
- In the process, the government promises a reduction in taxes to each taxpayer.

Theoretically, tax vouchers give all children the opportunity for a better education by facilitating educational choice, while at the same time decreasing the tax burden on the public. On the surface, it may seem that everybody wins!

What Really Happens . . .

In reality, what happens to those families who most need the opportunity for a better educational environment?

- Lower-income families cannot afford to pay the tuition and other costs for a non-public-funded education that are beyond the $1,500 tax voucher.
- The very people the voucher system is purported to serve are least able to take advantage of the option.

To the funding of public education?

- With the loss of each student the district loses the full amount of the state funding (in our example, the full $7,000).
- If you calculate the cost of one teaching position (salary and benefits) to be $70,000, the loss of just ten students equates to the elimination of one teacher.

To academic improvement?

- With reduced funding of the public school district, teachers are eliminated.
- With reduced funding of the public school district, class sizes increase.
- With reductions in the number of teachers and the increase in class sizes, academic achievement continues to decline.

To music programs?

- With a decline in funding for the public school district, cuts need to be made in educational services.
- Arts programs become a primary target for elimination because of reduced funding.
- Instrumental and vocal music (and arts) programs in the elementary schools are often cut first, leading to a collapse in secondary music programs.

The net results?

- Only families with sufficient income, who can afford to pay the difference in tuition for a private institution or costs for home schooling beyond the tax voucher amount, can take advantage of the voucher (which, in our case, was only $1,500).

- The quality of public education, particularly in areas of lower economic status, continues to decline.
- Property owners seem to gain most from the apparent per-student tax reductions (in our example, $5,500, the difference between the $7,000 per student cost and the $1,500 voucher) for each student removed from the district rolls. However, this assumes that the state actually implements a tax reduction, and does not spend any monies saved on other projects.
- There may be some advantage to proprietors of private music studios, since some states permit the use of tax vouchers to pay for individual lessons. In some cases, states or local districts have adopted policies that consider such lessons as fulfilling curriculum standards for a music education.
- Many students are deprived of the opportunity to participate in an adequate music education. These students are often those for whom it may have been most important.

As you can see, implementing a tax voucher system has the potential to polarize communities along social, economic, and ethnic divisions, leading to the deterioration of any concept of equal educational opportunities for children in our schools. For those of us who place high value on offering our children a complete education that includes music and arts curriculum offerings, tax voucher systems jeopardize these programs by siphoning essential community support away from our public school systems. Tax vouchers may provide improved educational opportunities, but those opportunities and benefits will only be for the few children whose families can afford to pay for them out of pocket.

For descriptions of policies enacted in several states, as well as further information and other perspectives on this issue, visit the Education Commission of the States website on tax vouchers at www.ecs.org/html/issue .asp?issueid=149.

SCHOOL TO WORK

The basic concept behind the school to work (STW) movement is that no student should leave school without a salable, marketable work skill. As is true with so many educational reform movements, there are some good basic foundational ideas. It is difficult to disagree with the concept that everyone who graduates from high school should be able to get a job. However, as is also true with similar proposals, there are some pitfalls. Many times this depends on how each state or district implements the plan.

With STW, the students make an early career choice by selecting a track (option) for their high school education. They then take the courses that are part of that track, somewhat similar to selecting a major in college. They receive their training during the high schools years and enter the market-place upon graduation.

Who Benefits?

Property owners and businesses that:

- receive the theoretical tax breaks;
- receive taxpayer-funded job training for potential employees;
- pay lower salaries because potential employees do not have a college education;
- may receive government grants for businesses that participate;
- have liability insurance coverage for students doing internships funded by the district;
- hope to eliminate the need for welfare systems.

Who Loses?

The school district, which:

- loses all funding if not in corpliance;
- must continue mandated programs when state and/or federal funding is discontinued;
- pays the cost of liability insurance for student internships.

The students, who:

- must select their career track as early as grade 8;
- if they decide to change career tracks, must take additional courses re-quired in the new track;
- are paid lower salaries because of lack of college education, although training may be similar;
- are from ethnic or economic groups against whom these programs discriminate;
- no longer are permitted to participate in music, because it is not viewed as an option for those students in vocational technical pro-grams;
- no longer have the opportunity for a balanced and equal education;
- no longer receive an adequate preparation for functioning in a world economy or global society.

School to work has been adopted by several states. I have worked with two major situations, one statewide, in which the plan had been implemented or was under consideration. The design of both programs was highly discriminatory against ethnic minorities and families with low incomes. Coincidently, both programs under consideration were being led by people in the best position to end up with the jobs leading those programs.

See www.ed.gov/ and search for "school to work."

SCHEDULING: A CASE STUDY

One of the major areas of reform that seems to be ever with us is the subject of scheduling. It can take many forms, including the following:

- Traditional (six-, seven-, and eight-period options)
- Block scheduling

  o Middle school blocks (exploratories, wheels)
  o High school blocks
  o Three- and four-period blocks (3 x 3, 4 x 4, A/B forms, etc.)
  o Split schedules ("Skinnies")

- Rotating schedules (seven- and eight-period forms)
- Modular scheduling
- Zero hours (before- and after-school forms)

Sometimes proposals for scheduling changes may be combined with other reform movements or changes made within a school district.

Common Reasons for Proposals to Change Scheduling

Among other reasons, people may suggest changes to emphasize certain curricular areas and to improve test scores (math, science, reading, etc.). This often serves to also de-emphasize curricular areas perceived to have lesser or minimal academic importance (such as the arts). Sometimes proposals for scheduling reforms occur in times of financial crisis as well.

In my experience, however, one of the primary motivators is what I refer to as the agent of change crisis. In every instance where I have been contacted about scheduling reform, there has been an individual leading that change who is either new to the district or a key candidate for advancement to another position within the district. It appears that in order to develop an appropriate resume as an educational leader one must be perceived as an innovator or agent of change.

Guiding Principles of Decision Making

Regardless of whether the proposed change is perceived as positive or negative, these principles must be part of the decision-making process:

- The impact on the student must remain the primary concern.
- The community must be involved in the process to ensure student-centered decisions.
- It is the responsibility of the individual or group advocating the change to demonstrate scientific evidence that documents potential positive results of student achievement to be brought about by the change.
- It is not the responsibility of the community to prove that the change may or will be negative, although you will be wise to have all the evidence together to support your position.
- Remember—the environment of change may provide an opportunity for you to improve or expand opportunities for students to make music.
- Keep an open mind. Listen; understand; contribute. Ask questions that will clarify understanding (yours and theirs). Don't make accusations.

Asking the Right Questions Helps Keep the Focus on Meeting Student Needs

Educational reforms may be proposed at any time—and for reasons that are not always obvious. Even before reforms are suggested, it makes good sense to be prepared. Here are some general questions to help you move through the process of determining possible motivations for change and whether or not change is needed.

Who is leading the reform effort?

- A specific administrator or level of administration
- A specific area(s) of the curriculum (math, science, etc.)
- A movement within the community (back-to-basics, etc.)
- Legislative mandates

Why is change being sought?

- To balance the budget
- To eliminate teachers
- To raise test scores
- To create more options for students
- To reduce or increase class sizes
- To increase student time on task

- To reduce discipline problems
- To reduce student transfers to schools outside the district
- To reduce drop-out rates
- To reduce the frantic pace of the day
- To improve student achievement—if so, in what skill or subject?
- To meet the demands of increasing graduation requirements
- To promote the passing of a levy referendum
- To eliminate the grades 9 and 10 scheduling bottleneck
- Due to the current political climate

How will the decision impact the ability of students to make music?

- Will students be able to participate in more than one music group (band, choir, and/or orchestra)?
- Will single-section courses be scheduled in conflict with music courses or with private or group lesson programs?
- Will music be required to move outside the school day to an extra-curricular classification?
- Will fees be added for continued participation in music?
- Will the school be able to offer a diverse curriculum that includes smaller music class options such jazz ensembles, madrigal singers, and AP theory?
- Will music classes meet daily?
- Will students be able to participate in music performance classes for the entire year?
- Do you have adequate facilities to provide for continuing all your music courses?
- How will staffing be impacted—reduced, increased, teaching teams?
- How will the various and specific lines of the music budget be affected?
- Can you list all the possible positive outcomes for music students?
- Can you list all the possible negative outcomes for music students?

Is there a system of assessment in place to demonstrate the potential success or failure of the proposed change?

As we begin to analyze how school day schedules change with each of the various educational reform movements, keep in mind the basic concepts and guiding questions presented above. I will share several scenarios with you that at times may seem unbelievable, but each example is based on situations that have actually occurred in school districts.

As proposals to change schedules emerge in your school district, you can assume the following to be true:

- There will be adult- and student-centered issues.
- Your district's contract with the teacher's union will have a major impact on the decision-making process.
- While improvement in student achievement may appear to be the central focus of the issue, the proposed change may have little or no positive impact on improving the environment for learning. Improving the situation for teachers does not necessarily ensure a positive result for students.
- Community members are apt to be left out of the process, unless advocates of the music coalition stay informed and get actively involved.

In examining the various scheduling options, you will learn to implement effective procedures and ask the questions suggested previously to help resolve issues in your own district. You will begin to understand how the system works, and how you and your music coalition can become more effective as advocates. You'll be able to use the questions and examples offered to work for positive change in your own district, and you'll learn how to block efforts that may have long-term negative effects on student learning.

> The district has appointed a scheduling reform task force.
> Are you or any other members of your music coalition on it?
> If not, ask to be on the task force, or at least attend the meetings.

The Traditional Six-Period Schedule

Let's start with the traditional six-period day. Most of us have at least a working understanding of this standard model, so it's a good baseline to use for comparison when examining other scheduling options.

We'll use the following basic assumptions about one model district—let's call it the Central School District—in this series of sections on educational reform movements.

- Central provides 180 instructional days per year. Did you ever wonder why no one calls them "learning days?" This is a perfect way to highlight the difference between an adult-centered and student-centered approach.
- The district operates on a two-semester academic year (ninety instructional days per semester).
- The high school currently operates with a six-period day.
- There are 355 minutes in the school day.
- The student has the option of taking six classes per day.

- There are five minutes between each period, or twenty-five minutes per day of "passing" time.
- There are 330 minutes of instructional time per day, or 55 minutes per course.
- There are 9,900 minutes of instructional time per (1 credit) course over the academic year.
- According to the district contract the teacher provides instruction for five periods each day, with the sixth period as a preparatory hour.
- Teacher instructional time per day is 275 minutes.
- Teacher preparatory time is fifty-five minutes.
- The high school is a four-year grade alignment with students in grades 9–12.
- The schedule provides for 24 credits of classes during four years of high school, with a full-year course receiving 1 credit, and a single-semester course receiving .5 credit.

Here are a few additional thoughts to remember.

- Reform may not just be a music issue; it may have a negative effect on other areas of the curriculum as well.
- How you act during the process may determine your effectiveness or ineffectiveness in future issues that arise in the district.
- Change for the sake of change is just that—change!
- Are there factors in the proposal that may help you improve your music program?

The Process Is Set in Motion

Now that we have defined the basic six-period traditional scheduling model for the Central School District, the district has just proposed changing to seven- or eight-period days. What will that mean to the students and teachers in the district?

Scheduling Myths and the Grades 9 and 10 Bottleneck

Complaints from students and parents about the grades 9 and 10 bottleneck had increased to the point where the district could no longer ignore them. It was one of the primary motivators for considering the schedule change. If you're not familiar with it, the term *bottleneck* is often used to refer to a school system's tendency to require too many courses in grades 9 and 10, particularly courses that must be taken in a four-year sequence. Students often are given the impression they must drop elective subjects like music.

Several issues were at the root of the problem, and holding on to beliefs in some common myths were now preventing officials from addressing the bottleneck effectively.

Raising Test Scores

Due to the provisions of the No Child Left Behind Act and similar legislative directives, there had been a growing demand to raise test scores over the last several decades, leading to an (over)emphasis on math, science, and reading. This district responded to public and legislative pressure by increasing graduation requirements in math, science, and in some cases reading.

> *Myth #1*: Increasing requirements in a particular curriculum area will result in higher test score results.
> *Fact*: In some cases (California, for example) the ever-increasing emphasis on the "basics" (reading, math, and science) seems to have had the opposite result.
> *Myth #2*: Participation in perceived nonessential courses such as music is detrimental to student achievement in other areas of the curriculum.
> *Fact*: Research indicates students participating in the arts seem to be achieving the highest results, as affirmed by results on the SAT and other tests.

World Language Requirements

There is a strong movement advocating the requirement of a minimum of two years of a world language. Isn't music one of those?

> *Myth #3*: (All) universities are now requiring a minimum of two years of world language for admission.
> *Fact*: While it is true that some universities have adopted that requirement, most universities only require students to fulfill language requirements to obtain their undergraduate degree (meaning students can meet the language requirement during their course of college study).

Computer Literacy and Physical Education

Two other catalysts for proposing the scheduling change were the demand for computer literacy and increased requirements for physical education.

> *Myth #4*: Physical education (PE) is a required course for grades 9 and 10.
> *Fact*: Physical education credits are graduation requirements. They are normally scheduled in grade 9 and 10 as a tradition, from the desire to

fulfill the requirement early so the student can participate in varsity athletics, and/or as a means of getting the requirement "out of the way." Scheduling PE classes during the junior and senior years can serve to alleviate the bottleneck.

Myth #5: Computer literacy courses are more marketable and therefore more important to students than music or arts courses.

Fact: While it's certainly true that young people today need to be computer savvy, there is a significant body of research (see www.supportmusic .com) about the value of music as preparation for the twenty-first-century workplace. Business leaders and other employers place high value on qualities such as teamwork, concentration, creativity, problem-solving abilities, and more—all the skills used by dedicated music students!

The administration in one district suggested solving the scheduling problem by dividing band, choir, and orchestra students into two groups. It was suggested that group A take music during the fall semester and PE during the spring semester. Group B would then take PE fall semester and music spring semester. Then they could all "go back into music" together the sophomore year. Fortunately, that proposal was perceived by nearly everyone as ludicrous. This district initially resolved the grade 9 bottleneck by advising those students to schedule PE during their junior or senior year.

No Need for Music

Some guidance counselors were even advising students to drop their participation in music, because the student "wasn't going to be a professional musician."

Myth #6: Music is just entertainment and not really important to students.

Fact: Research reveals strong correlations between quality music education in school and academic achievement, healthy social development, and general quality of life.

Despite these facts, it appeared that officials of Students Central still believed many of these myths, so they were going to consider some various approaches to scheduling reform. Because of their current financial constraints and contract with the teachers' union, the school board had made several assumptions as it began the process:

- Budgetary limitations required that any change have minimal effect on the district's anticipated fund balance.
- The length of the school day (for teachers) would not change.

- The school year would continue to be 180 teaching days (90 per semester).
- The length of the school day for 1.0 FTE teacher would continue at a maximum of 330 minutes.
- The district needed to provide some way to increase the number of credits a student may take during his or her four years in high school.

Two Options for Seven-Period Scheduling

The meeting of the Schedule Task Force of the Central School District was called to order, and the week's agenda dealt with two proposals to resolve the various issues related to scheduling, in particular the lack of a scheduling structure that facilitates adequate curricular offering to meet the needs of the student.

Members were introduced and asked to share their role on the task force. Music advocates were pleased to see that the administration did an adequate job of ensuring representation by various constituents of the district—one member was specifically chosen to represent the Central School District Music Coalition and the chair of the music department also served on the committee. Several other people on the schedule task force were also members of the music coalition, but their official roles were to represent specific schools or boundary areas in the district, senior citizens, and the teachers' union.

The district reviewed the issues of the scheduling problem and several assumptions that had been adopted by the board, and then presented the task force with two options for moving to a seven-period day. Basically, moving to a seven-period schedule could be accomplished in one of two ways: by increasing the school day by an extra hour or by adding the extra period without lengthening the school day.

The task force was divided into two groups. Each group was asked to develop pros and cons for one of the options. Here's a summary of their results.

Option 1: Add One Hour to the School Day

Pros

- Students would have more flexibility in their schedule.
- Periods would continue to be the same length (fifty-five minutes).
- Students would be able to take twenty-eight credits during the four years of high school, resolving the issue of increased graduation requirements and the scheduling bottleneck problem for the near future.

Cons

- The length of the school day would be increased by sixty minutes, which could cause a problem with after-school activities.
- Since the current contract with the teachers' union called for a maximum number of teaching minutes and classes taught per day, the contract would need to be renegotiated, or a significant number of additional teachers hired.
- Since it was unlikely that the union would add another period to the current teaching load, it was probable that this plan was not financially feasible unless the district held a levy referendum asking voters to fund the increased costs of hiring new teachers to provide instruction for the additional period. (Note: In some cases a district may use a process like this to establish a basis to call for a levy referendum. The resolution of a major problem for students is often a significant motivator for the "yes" voter.)

Option 2: Divide the Six Periods into Seven

Pros

- Students would have more flexibility in their schedule.
- The length of the school day would not change.
- Students would be able to take twenty-eight credits during the four years of high school, resolving the issue of increased graduation requirements and the scheduling bottleneck problem for the near future.
- Increases in costs appeared to be minimal, if the teachers' union would agree to teach a sixth period (six out of seven). This may have been possible, since the number of teaching minutes required daily to teach six periods would increase by only one minute.

Cons

- The length of individual periods would be reduced from fifty-five minutes to forty-six minutes, significantly decreasing the students' time on task.
- While the number of teaching minutes would remain basically the same (assuming the teachers were to teach six periods per day), the student load of the teacher would increase by thirty students. It is unlikely that the union would accept this without major financial adjustments. If the union would not agree to the additional period of instruction (even though the number of minutes remained basically the same), then the increase in costs would be similar to option 1.

The Outcome: Examine Further Options

To members of the task force, it was evident that the cons of both options 1 and 2 outweighed the pros. In general, option 1 was preferred over option 2 due to the concern of the shortened class period. The task force was also realistic about the issue of the additional costs of option 1. Members of the task force agreed that other options should be discussed and then introduced three additional suggestions for discussion at the next meeting:

1. One parent suggested that moving to a seven-period day was a short-sighted option, and thought it would be better to consider an eight-period day. This would offer students the possibility of achieving thirty-two credits during the four years of high school and allow students to receive a much broader education.
2. A second individual suggested that it might be possible to resolve some of the negative issues raised about the two seven-period options presented in this meeting by examining a rotating schedule.
3. One of the administrators (new to the district) was quick to add that the district could resolve all of the scheduling issues if they adopted a block schedule format.

Discussion on all three suggestions was tabled, and the administration was charged with examining the feasibility of each at future meetings of the Task Force.

Agenda for the Next Meeting: Eight-Period Day and Rotating Schedule

The agenda for the next meeting focused on suggestions number 1 and 2 above, and the administration was asked to make a presentation on block schedules at the subsequent meeting.

At this meeting, it was determined that one or more of the scheduling reform options discussed must be eliminated as not feasible. The executive committee felt this was necessary to allow the task force to achieve its primary mission to facilitate a change in schedule.

Option 3: The Eight-Period Day

The first item on the agenda was the eight-period day (within the current length of day of 355 minutes). After a short discussion it became obvious that the pros and cons of the eight-period day were similar to those of the seven-period day. The overriding problem with this proposal was the reduction of class period length to forty minutes. The proposal to switch to an eight-period day was eliminated from further consideration by consent, with the recommendation that it be considered as an option within the concept of a rotating schedule. It was also noted that an eight-period day might be a more viable option at the middle school level.

The task force then divided into two separate committees to determine the issues related to the adoption of a rotating schedule; one committee was assigned the seven-period rotation, and the other discussed the eight-period rotation.

The Rotating Schedule: Pros and Cons

The aim of a rotating schedule is to provide scheduling flexibility while minimizing or eliminating the loss of instructional time. It is often used to assure there are minimal changes to existing contracts between the teachers' union and the district.

Option 4: The Seven-Period Rotation

In this format only six periods of the full seven-period schedule meet on any given day, according to the following eight-day rotation schedule:

Day 1: periods 1–6
Day 2: periods 2–7
Day 3: periods 3–1
Day 4: periods 4–2
Day 5: periods 5–3
Day 6: periods 6–4
Day 7: periods 7–5
Day 8: periods 1–6 (begins the second rotation)

Potential confusion about daily schedules would be eliminated with a sign at each entrance to the building indicating what day it was or, in other words, which period begins that day. If the sign said, "Today is Day 3," then the first class period of the day is period 3 and the last period of the day is period 1. Each period meets six out of seven days. Experience indicated that while it may take a short time for adults to adjust to this concept, students have little difficulty with the transition.

Pros

- Students would have more flexibility in their schedule.
- Periods would continue to be the same length (fifty-five minutes).
- The length of the school day would not change.

- Students would be able to take twenty-eight credits during the four years of high school, resolving the issue of increased graduation requirements and the scheduling bottleneck for the near future.

Cons

- While the length of class periods would remain the same, there would be fewer class meetings per year.
- The negative effect of lost periods would probably result in lowering student mastery of skills.

Undetermined Outcomes

- If teachers continued to teach only five of seven periods, the prep time per rotation would increase to 110 minutes. Depending on the actual schedule of the individual teacher there would be some days when the teacher had the full 110 minutes of prep time, and other days when the teacher had only one prep hour. There would be a net gain of 55 minutes of prep time per rotation.
- If teachers were asked to teach six of the seven periods per rotation, teaching time would be increased by fifty-five minutes per rotation.
- If teachers did not teach the sixth class per rotation, this option would create the need to hire a significant number of additional teachers, causing increases in demands on the budget.

Option 5: The Eight-Period Rotation

Implementation of this schedule would be similar to that in the seven-period rotation. The daily schedule would continue to include six periods of fifty-five minutes each. However, it would now take eight days to complete one rotation. Each period would meet six out of eight days.

Pros

- Students would have more flexibility in their schedule.
- Periods would continue to be the same length (fifty-five minutes).
- The length of the school day would not change.
- Students would be able to take thirty-two credits during the four years of high school, resolving the issue of increased graduation requirements and the scheduling bottleneck for the near future.
- While teachers would be asked to teach six out of eight periods, they would also be given two prep hours per rotation. This would be a much more viable option for the teachers' union.

- No additional teachers would need to be hired, assuming the teachers' union agreed to the change.

Cons

- While the length of class periods would remain the same, there would be fewer class meetings per year.
- The negative effect of lost periods would probably result in lowering student mastery of skills.

Decision Time on Scheduling Options to Date

As determined earlier, the task force meeting ended with a discussion of the various options presented thus far and decided to eliminate the following options:

- The eight-period day (option 3): Eliminated earlier in the meeting. It would reduce class period time to forty minutes.
- The seven-period day, with fifty-five-minute classes (option 1): Eliminated. It was not a financially viable or realistic option because it would extend the length of the school day.
- The seven-period rotation (option 4): Eliminated. It was not a financially viable or realistic option because it would require significant alteration to the teachers' contract and the hiring of additional teachers, making it less appealing than the eight-period rotation.

The following options were kept on the table for continued discussion:

- The seven-period day, with classes reduced to forty-six minutes each (option 2)
- The eight-period rotation (option 5)

The Block Schedule

Adding a Music Education Advocacy Perspective to a Block Schedule

At the close of the meeting, everyone was reminded that the administration would present its proposal to move to a block schedule at the next regular task force meeting. Two other items were quickly presented before adjournment.

1. One parent suggested that the committee was spending a lot of time on the issue of scheduling, and expressed concern that the committee needed some time to redefine the issues. Following a brief discussion,

one specific request for information emerged: "How many students are actually affected by the limitations of the six-period day?" The administration indicated it would report its findings at the next task force meeting.

2. In anticipation of the administration's upcoming block schedule presentation, the representative from the music coalition requested a preliminary meeting with the administration prior to the next regular meeting of the task force to discuss the coalition's preliminary research on the block schedule and potential music issues. This would allow the administration to include any relevant information from those discussions in the block schedule presentation.

The Value of Privacy

Members of the music coalition requested this private task force subcommittee meeting for the following reasons:

- The music teachers and the music coalition had reviewed the research on the effects of block schedule on music curriculum, and had found a potential for both positive and negative impacts on the music program.
- The music coalition decided to address its initial concerns in a private forum to avoid the appearance of public confrontation, and because it didn't want to place the administration in an embarrassing position before the rest of the schedule task force.
- The music coalition desired to maintain a collaborative decision-making process to enhance communication and foster a positive long-term problem solving relationship with the administration.
- The music coalition wanted to consider potential improvements in the music program, as well as to ensure that the potential adoption of a block schedule format met the basic needs identified for survival of the program.

What Is Block Scheduling?

Block Scheduling is used to increase student "time on task" by lengthening each of the class periods; it is sometimes referred to as semestering. Block scheduling reduces daily instruction to four (extended) periods as opposed to the traditional six-period school day. With the increased time on task, students are able to complete course requirements in a particular subject area in one semester instead of a full year. Using a block schedule, students can complete the equivalent of eight courses (as opposed to six) in the same number of school days per year. An alternate form of block scheduling is typically referred to as the A/B format. In this model classes meet for an entire year, but on alternate days. In both cases the number of class sessions is reduced by 50 percent.

Block Scheduling and the Music Student

The music coalition first presented four primary concerns and requested each of them be considered. Before any scheduling format was adopted, it must:

- Facilitate student participation in music for the entire year
- Provide for additional staffing as necessary to make sure that curricular diversity was not reduced
- Allow for student participation in more than one music class
- Minimize scheduling conflicts for the student

During discussions, and keeping in mind the above student needs, it became clear that the music program could experience potential benefits or negative outcomes. Here is a summary of the group's findings.

Pros

- The increased number of minutes available in each class period could facilitate additional curricular content in music performance (band, choir, and orchestra) classes, such as music theory, music history, listening, student conducting, and improvisation.
- Longer rehearsals could help develop the endurance required in a public performance, particularly as the dates of concerts approached.

Cons

- There could be negative reactions to the number of music credits students could accumulate over a four-year period and apply to graduation requirements (up to 25 percent of the total).
- There was research indicating a tendency for increased student attrition with the implementation of block schedule.
- Increased scheduling conflicts were likely when the students have only four periods per day rather than six.
- There could be a loss of curricular options in music. In the traditional six-period day the teacher provides five periods of instruction, or potentially five different courses. In the block schedule the teacher teaches only three periods. Therefore, the students could potentially have their curricular options in music reduced by two (40 percent).

- If the district promised no reduction in curricular diversity they would need to provide additional positions to teach those courses that would otherwise no longer be offered. Therefore, there could be increased costs due to the need to hire additional teachers to maintain curricular options for students. This would be true in other subject areas as well.

At the conclusion of the meeting, music coalition members distributed copies of the research studies they cited during their presentation and a summary of the talking points they had mentioned. The administration thanked the music coalition members for their input and seemed particularly pleased to have some information to digest and refer to after the meeting. The administration representatives said they would take these factors into consideration when they presented their proposal at the next regular schedule task force meeting.

The Administrative Proposal

Two Options for Four-Period Block Scheduling

After calling the next meeting of the schedule task force to order, the administration distributed a large packet of information in support of its proposal to adopt a block schedule format.

The administration started by reminding members about the initial goals of the task force, and then suggested that research showed adopting the block schedule would be the best way to meet these goals.

Research Claims about Block Schedule

During their presentation, the administration showed research to indicate block scheduling would:

- Eliminate the bottleneck by allowing students to enroll in eight courses per year.
- Allow students to earn up to thirty-two credits during the four years they are enrolled in high school.
- Allow students to potentially fulfill the minimum requirements for graduation (twenty-four credits) in only three years by taking eight credits each year.
- Increase "time on task" by expanding each class period from fifty-five to eighty-five minutes.
- Increase test scores because of increased "time on task."
- Increase graduation rates (reduce drop-outs) because of increased student success.
- Improve grades in the general student population.

When they finished outlining the basic research about block schedules, the administrators in favor of this schedule format outlined two options to implement a four-period block schedule.

Option 6a: The 4 x 4 Block Schedule

- Students would take up to four courses per semester (eight per year).
- Each course would meet daily for eighty-five minutes.
- Each course would fulfill the requirements of a (previous) full-year course.
- "Skinnies" could be implemented for courses outside the (perceived) core, such as music and other electives and including courses like band, choir, and orchestra that need to meet for an entire year. (Note: A "skinny" is half of an eighty-five-minute period.)

Option 6b: The A/B Block Schedule

- Students would take up to eight courses per year. (Some districts require the students to take one study hall, allowing only seven courses per year.)
- Each course would meet every other day (A/B) for eighty-five minutes for the entire year.
- Each course would be considered as fulfilling the requirements of a (previous) full-year course.

Similarities between the Two Options

- A course that was previously meeting daily for a full year (one credit) would have the number of sessions reduced by 50 percent. For example, a course previous meeting for 180 days would be reduced to ninety sessions whether it was semesterized (4 x 4 block) or met on alternate days (A/B block).
- The length of the day would remain at 355 minutes, but students would only pass between classes three times instead of four. Therefore, the extra ten minutes gained would be added to class time.
- A teacher's load would be reduced from five fifty-five-minute periods per day to three eighty-five-minute periods per day.
- A teacher's load would increase from five courses per year to six courses per year.
- A teacher's daily student load would be decreased.

Controversy and No Decision

From the beginning of the meeting it was evident that this proposal was going to be controversial. In addition to the preliminary research done by the music coalition, other task force members had done their own research, scouring the Internet for information related to block schedules.

There seemed to be a general sense that block schedules were where the administration was headed from the very beginning. Some individuals even expressed concern privately that the task force had been appointed as a "rubber stamp committee" and that, even though the administration and board had involved the community, they intended to decide in favor of block scheduling regardless of public opinion or concerns. Even the teachers seemed divided over the concept.

Discussion on the two options was extensive and lengthy, but no clear recommendations emerged. Therefore, it was decided that there would be a second meeting on the topic of block scheduling, with the task force divided into subcommittees according to the two options. People were asked to go to their various constituencies with the information, do their own research, and then come to the next meeting ready to present specific summary reports and comments on the two options.

Three Perspectives on Block Scheduling

At the previous meeting of the scheduling task force, members listened to the administration's presentation and recommendation to adopt one of two forms of block scheduling. This week, the task force members planned to divide into two groups to discuss the pros and cons of the two block scheduling options (4 x 4 and A/B).

However, the intensity of the discussions that concluded the last meeting had increased significantly since that time. The growing divisions within the task force had now polarized to the point that everyone decided it would be a good idea to divide into three study groups for the meeting. Each of the three groups—administrators, teachers, and members of the community— was charged with making a recommendation about whether or not the district should adopt the 4 x 4 or A/B form of the block schedule.

Here's an eye-opening summary of their differing perspectives.

The Administrative Team

Members of the administrative team spent much of their time and energy reorganizing the approach to their proposal and emphasizing key research highlights. They decided it was most important to focus on the following points.

- Elimination of the scheduling bottleneck
- Increasing "time on task" to increase test scores
- Increasing graduation rates (reducing attrition)
- Less classes to schedule per day to reduce the load of guidance counselors

- Reduction of discipline problems, because students would spend less time in the hallways between classes

They decided to maintain their position that adopting one of the block schedule formats would be best for the district.

The Teachers

Teacher representatives summarized their support of the recommendation to adopt one of the block scheduling formats by emphasizing the following factors.

- Teachers would have less students and classes per day, allowing them to devote more attention to individual student needs.
- Teachers would have more students and classes per year, providing fiscal viability.
- Teachers would have increased prep time, enabling them to spend more time developing their materials.

Generally speaking, the teachers also decided to support block scheduling, even though some of them agreed with some points made by opponents to the block schedule at the last meeting.

The Community

The study group that included members of the community had quite a different approach. It seemed that most of the research and materials presented on block scheduling had addressed positive aspects of the effects block scheduling would have on administrators and teachers. Much of their rationale appeared to be based the assumption that "what is good for teachers (or the institution) is good for students."

The members of the community used the approach that "what is good for students is good for the institution." With every issue discussed, they asked, "What will the impact be on the student?" (Note: It should be stated here that several members of the community worked for corporations in which they were dealing with issues of human resources in their own occupations. Consequently, they had done much of their own research on the subject.)

Another Perspective on the Research

Community members first noted that the massive amounts of data distributed by the administration, and available via the Internet and other resources, had one primary common characteristic: in over sixty years of use, there was no significant scientific evidence or data that indicated positive short- or long-term growth in overall student achievement or standardized test results.

Though there was some evidence that graduation rates increased and grades improved, information released by the College Board and the Advanced Placement (AP) Testing Service appeared to substantiate the evidence of the negative impact of block scheduling on student performance. In responding to poor student performance in states or districts with the greatest number of schools that had adopted block scheduling, they stated, "Students who completed year-long AP courses offered only in the fall or spring have tended to perform poorly on the examinations." These sources further stated, "The majority of AP teachers, coordinators, readers, and test development committee members opposed block scheduling." And finally, the College Board suggested, "There is a need for controlled, longitudinal studies of the impact of block scheduling upon learning" (Office of Regional Affairs, College Board, July 14, 1998).

One of the members of the community serving on the task force developed the data in table 7.2 to provide information that had either been disregarded or unavailable in previous meetings.

Community members provided the following summary of some of the more significant administrative and teacher issues revealed in the comparison between traditional and block schedule concepts.

- Although it is true there would be fewer courses to schedule, there would be increased potential for schedule conflict because of the reduction from six to only four periods per day.
- Although it is true that teachers would have fewer students and classes per day, there would be an increase in the number of teachers on prep

Table 7.2 Comparison of Traditional and Block Schedules

	Traditional: 6 periods	Block: 4 x 4 or A/B
Length of School Day	355 minutes	355 minutes
Student Class Load	6 classes per day	4 classes per day
Length of Class Periods	55 minutes	85 minutes
Sessions per Course	180	90
Average Class Size	30	32.5
Daily Student Class Time	330 minutes	340 minutes
Between-Class Time	25 minutes (5 x 5)	15 minutes (3 x 5)
Teacher Class Load	5 classes per day	3 classes per day
Teaching Time per Day	275 minutes	255 minutes
Class Time per Course	9,900 minutes	7,650 minutes

time during any given period (one out of four per period instead of one out of six). Therefore, the district would either need to increase class sizes by an average of 8 percent or hire additional teachers to keep classes at the current level of thirty students.

- The district could make certain elective teaching positions half-time. For example, a language teacher providing three levels of instruction (e.g., Spanish I, II, and III) could be required to schedule those courses only in the fall semester.
- Although it is true the "time on task" per period would increase from fifty-five to eighty-five minutes, the semesterizing of instruction would require teachers to cover two days of class materials per period. This would not be likely to happen when the length of the class period would be increased by only thirty minutes. In fact, many teachers had clearly stated they did not attempt to cover as much material in a course in the block schedule format. Further, many provided a short "mental break" in the middle of the lengthy period, or even treated the last part of the period as a study hall. (Little wonder the research indicated this was a popular format with students, or that graduation rates improved.)
- When comparing data, the time a teacher spent in class per day was reduced by twenty minutes while, at the same time, teachers gained thirty minutes for the prep hour, gaining a total of fifty minutes non-teaching time per day. (Little wonder that block scheduling was a popular format with many teachers. One teacher even stated, "Why should I complain? I have fewer classes and students, and got a raise in pay!")

While most members of the committee were greatly disturbed by the data related to administrative and teacher issues, there was even greater distress over the following potential negative affects on students, summarized below.

- There would be increases in class size.
- There would be a potential for greater scheduling conflicts (particularly in the 4 x 4 format), because of the decrease in the number of periods per day.
- There would be occasional major gaps between classes (particularly in the A/B format), because of holidays or other nonteaching days that normally fall on a Monday.
- There could be major gaps between certain courses (again, particularly in the 4 x 4 format). For example, a student taking Spanish I in fall semester one year might not be able to take Spanish II until the next fall.
- In any curricular area where there was only one instructor, the reduction of the teaching load from five courses to three courses would

cause a 40 percent loss of curricular options, unless an additional instructor was hired to cover those courses. This would obviously add a
significant cost factor to the district budget.

- The major issue, however, was the loss of instructional time per student. With each course meeting for one semester, the number of class
days per course would be reduced from 180 to 90. In the traditional
six-period day, a 55-minute class meets 180 times for a total of 9,900
minutes. Under the block schedule format, an 85-minute class meets
only 90 times, for a total of 7,650 minutes. This loss of 2,250 minutes
of instructional time is equivalent to a loss of eight weeks of instructional time per course for the student. In sequential courses such as
algebra that cover two years on a traditional system, a total of sixteen
weeks of instructional time would be lost. To achieve full mastery of
subject competencies, some districts had added new course requirements for graduation to make up for lost time in those curricular areas
(e.g., Algebra III). Therefore, the proposed advantage of offering more
course options (electives) with block scheduling was minimized or
eliminated.

The community study group took a verbal straw vote and nearly all members expressed a negative vote against the adoption of either form of block
scheduling.

The Groups Report to Each Other

Having completed their efforts, the various study groups came back together to report their findings. After the administrative and teacher groups
shared their information, the community group summarized its findings
and distributed copies of their comparison of traditional and block schedules (see table 7.2) to show the weaknesses in the block schedule format.
They then clearly expressed their position of nonsupport for either form.

After considerable discussion, it became evident that several of the teachers (particularly in the traditional core areas of mathematics, reading, and
the sciences) had the same reservations. By the end of the meeting there was
no significant support or mandate for the administrative recommendation
to adopt the block schedule.

Where Do We Go From Here?

Upon further discussion a subcommittee made up of members of each of
the three subgroups (administration, teachers, and community) was appointed to develop a chart similar to the comparison of traditional and
block schedules in table 7.2 in which all the various scheduling formats

were compared. This information would be distributed to the task force for study before the next meeting. This chart would provide the basis for moving ahead in attempting to fulfill the task force charge of facilitating scheduling reform in the district.

At the conclusion of the meeting, someone once again raised the question, "How many students does the ninth and tenth grade bottleneck really affect?" The administrative reported its findings that only about 10 percent of the students were affected by the current scheduling bottleneck. It appeared, therefore, that adoption of the block schedule would place approximately 90 percent of the students in the position of taking a study hall (see "The Study Hall Game" in chapter 8), a position that was neither educationally or financially viable. (In fact, some districts that have adopted the block require that a student take at least one study hall as part of their eight courses per year).

Someone else responded, "Isn't there some kind of solution that could address the needs of that 10 percent of the students without forcing 100 percent of the students into a structure that was either ineffective or unworkable?" Someone else said, "Why not offer the choice of an optional seventh period for those students who are facing the scheduling bottleneck?"

Everyone decided that the next meeting of the task force would feature two agenda items:

1. A summary of the comparison of key aspects of the various scheduling formats
2. An administrative report on the feasibility of an optional seventh period for students confronted by the scheduling bottleneck.

Decision Time!

At the previous meeting of the scheduling task force, a subcommittee was asked to compare and contrast the key issues of seven scheduling options.

They developed an informative and convenient table summarizing the main issues and also shared some important observations to help everyone analyze all the information.

As you look at table 7.3, pay careful attention to whether the issues are primarily adult-centered or student-centered.

Summary of Primary Observations

- Option 3: The eight-period day with an extended day and full fifty-five-minute periods was excluded as not feasible because of the minimal length of periods and extreme costs.

- Adding a full seventh period would lengthen the day for all students, require significant addition of teachers, and be the most expensive option.
- All options would reduce the number of minutes of instruction per course ("time on task"), except options 1 and 7.
- The rotating eight-period day and both forms of the block schedule would cause the greatest loss of student time per course, an equivalent of 9.4 and 8.2 weeks respectively.
- The block schedule formats appeared to offer the greatest advantages to teachers by reducing the teaching time per day, while at the same time increasing the length of the preparatory period. Further, some districts were requiring that students in the A/B format take one of their eight periods as a study hall Others were suggesting that the greatest majority of students would only sign up for six courses anyway, thereby being required to take two study halls per day (see "The Study Hall Game" in chapter 8).
- Both the seven- and eight-period options would lose "time on task" due to the reduction in the number of class meetings.
- All options appeared to resolve the ninth and tenth grade scheduling bottleneck, except for the current traditional six-period format.
- All options, except option 7, would have major negative effect(s) on students.

Following this presentation, the full task force engaged in a very student-centered discussion. Members turned their attention to whether or not it was possible to offer the option of an additional period prior to the beginning of the normal school day (option 7 in table 7.3). Since the subcommittee had anticipated this idea would be put on the table for discussion, members had already worked with the administration to gather the information needed to make a decision about its potential to solve the scheduling bottleneck.

"Zero" Hour or the Optional Seventh Period Solution

The implementation of a "zero" hour as an optional seventh period for students appeared to fulfill the original charge to the task force as established by the Board of Education: "Solve the problem of the ninth and tenth grade scheduling bottleneck."

Here are some of the issues discussed prior to the task force's final decision to recommend the zero hour option.

Issue 1: Budgetary Implications

The cost factor involved was limited to two primary issues: hiring of faculty to teach the zero hour and transportation. Since only 10 percent of the

Table 7.3 Summary Comparison of Traditional Six-Period Day and Options 1–7

Option / Adult/Student Issue	Current Traditional 6 Period	1 7 Period 415 Minutes	2 7 Period 355 Minutes	4 Rotate 7	5 Rotate 8	6 Block 4 x 4 or A/B	7 Zero Hour
Length of Day in Minutes	355	415	355	355	355	355	355/415
Periods per Day	6	7	7	6	6	4	7
Passing Minutes per Day	25	30	30	25	25	15	30
Daily Contract Minutes	330	385	325	330	330	340	330/385
Length of Periods	55 minutes	55 minutes	46 minutes	55 minutes	55 minutes	85 minutes	55 minutes
Teaching Periods Per Day or Rotation	5	5 of 7	5 of 7	5 of 7	6 of 8	3 of 4 6 of 8	5
Teaching Minutes per Day or Rotation	275	275	230	275	330	255	275
Prep Time Minutes per Day or Rotation	16.7%	16.7%	16.7%	28.5%	25%	25%	25%
Course Meetings per Year	180	180	180	154	135	90	180
Student Courses per Year Maximum	6	7	7	7	8	8	7
Graduation Credits Maximum	24	28	28	28	32	32	28
Schedule Conflict Odds	1:6	1:7	1:7	1:7	1:8	1:4	1:7
Class Size	30	30	30	30	30	32.5	30
Contact Time per Course	9,900 minutes	9,900 minutes	8,280 minutes	8,470 minutes	7,425 minutes	7,650 minutes	9,900 minutes
Minutes per Course vs. Traditional		No change	-1620	-1530	-2575	-2250	No change
Days Lost or Gained vs. Traditional		No change	-29	-28	-47	-41	No change
Weeks Lost or Gained vs. Traditional		No change	-5.8	-5.6	-9.4	-8.2	No change

(300) grade 9 students were confronted by the scheduling bottleneck, it would only require the addition of one teacher per high school to accommodate the approximately thirty students. This could be accomplished in one of two ways: by adding a .167 FTE overload factor (and equivalent additional pay) for one teacher per school, *or* by altering the schedule of one teacher to teach from "zero" hour through period 5 (periods 0 through 5, instead of 1 through 6). The experiment could be implemented the first year in grade 9 only, and then added to other grades as feasible.

(Tip: When you are dealing with large budgets where amounts are expressed in millions, cross off the last three digits to make it easier to work with and mentally grasp figures. In other words, think of $64,000,000 as $64,000,~~000~~. Therefore, paying a "bill" of $50,000 in a budget of $64,000,000 is comparable to paying a bill of $50,~~000~~ out of a budget of $64,000,~~000~~.)

Issue 2: Transportation Cost Implications

The cost factor for transportation was not expected to be a major problem. Budgetary allocations for the transportation fund are rarely as restricted as the general fund. In this district, an early bus was provided for students who chose to attend a zero hour class. Other means of transportation—parents (car pools) or older siblings who drive—could also be available for students.

Issue 3: Curricular Implications

If elective courses were placed in zero hour, task force members pointed out it could negate the possibility of participation by the students who most needed the option to meet graduation requirements. Therefore, it was decided that only standard core courses required of all students would be offered during the zero hour. This district decided to offer grade 9 social studies in zero hour.

It's Thumbs Up for Zero Hour!

Following further discussion, the task force voted nearly unanimously to recommend the optional seventh period for adoption by the school board. The school board received the task force recommendation and adopted it, by unanimous approval, to go into effect the next fall for ninth grade students at Central School District.

Zero hour turned out to be a very successful ongoing solution: it was instituted the following year for tenth grade students and no further scheduling changes have been needed since that time.

TRIMESTER SYSTEM AND YEAR-ROUND SCHOOLS

There are two other options that periodically emerge during discussions of scheduling reform. While there are comparatively few districts where these systems are being used, music education advocates do need to be aware of their potential impact on music programming.

The Trimester System

Historically speaking, dividing the academic year into trimesters seems to be a compromise between the traditional two-semester system and the block schedule. With the trimester system, the typical thirty-six-week school year is divided into three equal terms of twelve weeks. Full-year courses (thirty-six weeks under the traditional schedule) would be reduced to twenty-four weeks in length. One-semester courses (eighteen weeks under the traditional schedule) would be reduced to twelve weeks in length. The primary issues for the music program are similar to those in the block schedule.

The number of courses per day and the length of periods may be changed in an attempt to resolve a variety of issues. If your district is considering the trimester system, I recommend you use the information provided in the previous sections as your guide and develop similar data to compare and contrast the specific format that your district is considering.

Year-Round Schools

In the majority of school districts, the traditional school year is currently scheduled over a nine- or ten-month period. With the year-round concept, the school year is scheduled over the entire calendar year of twelve months.

This concept may be confusing at first because it may appear the intent is to increase the number of days that students spend in school. However, this is not the case. Students continue to have an academic year of approximately 180 days; however, the district will be providing instruction for an additional sixty days.

There are three primary motivations for the year-round system:

1. Scheduling classes over twelve months increases school capacity by one-third. For example, a school building with capacity for only 750 students can accommodate 1,000 students on a four-track system, because 250 students will be on vacation during any given track.
2. Scheduling classes over twelve months may be used to reduce class size. For example, a school with 1,000 students enrolled could reduce the number of students on campus at any given time to 750. This may also

be used to alleviate overcrowding of space. Under the year-round system, students are placed in groups known as tracks. If the district adopts a four-track system, students attend classes during three of the four tracks (terms). In other words, during any given track 75 percent of the students will be in classes and 25 percent of the students will be on vacation. In some schools there may be multiple tracks in operation; in others, there may be only a single track. Each method of implementation has its own complexities.

3. Working parents may be provided with more flexibility in scheduling vacations or other family events. In other cases, such as areas where much of the work is seasonal (e.g., agriculture), students may be able to schedule their time out of school to coincide with the need to assist with work in the family business.

How Does Year-Round Scheduling Affect School Music Programs?

Music education advocates should help others in their districts to carefully consider both the consequences and the motivations of year-round scheduling before this system is adopted. Here are a few key issues to target as you assess the effect year-round scheduling may have on your district's music programming.

- Additional staffing will be needed to provide instruction for the fourth track or term.
- Team teaching is often necessary to provide instructional "catch-up time" for students who were on vacation (off-track) during a previous track.
- If the district does not provide additional staffing or multiple tracks, students may be forced to drop music because of scheduling conflicts within a specific track.
- Curricular design and assessment must be configured to ensure that students do not miss significant segments in any learning sequence.
- The scheduling of music performances must be made with great care to ensure that the maximum number of students are able to participate.

CHANGE FOR THE SAKE OF CHANGE

Before completing this section on educational reform I want to make it clear that change may be necessary and in many cases result in positive outcomes. However, change just for the sake of change (or any of the other reasons mentioned in the section on reform) does *not* in any way guarantee improvement.

Change can also be very good! An environment for change can serve as a means of advancing your program. Personally, I have always maintained a list of all the changes that I would like to see made in programs with which I have been involved. Whenever I hear of discussions related to change I get my list out. I make sure that I get involved in the process so that I can facilitate positive changes to the programs with which I or my own children are involved. I encourage you to do the same!

8

Crisis Management: The Budget

UNDERSTANDING FTE

Simply put, FTE (full-time equivalent) is a measurement used to establish the financial value of the various positions in a school district. Understanding FTE will help you—the parents, teachers, and other advocates of school music programs—unravel some of the complexities of your school budget process. The terms and concepts presented here are the building blocks used (or, in some cases, neglected) by administrators and school board members as they decide where monies should be allocated and where cuts will be made. Though this "insider" information may seem a little daunting at first, you too can learn to speak the language of your school's administrators and board members.

Bottom line? If you understand FTE—as it relates to individuals and positions, as well as programs—you'll be a stronger advocate for expansion or preservation of your school music program.

What Is FTE and Why Is It So Important?

FTE stands for *full-time equivalent*, or one (1.0) full-time teaching position. Your school defines each FTE position by a job classification or category (teacher, administrator, staff, etc.). The definition of 1.0 FTE is based on the district contract and input from your local teachers' organization.

How Do You Calculate FTE?

You can calculate the FTE of any teacher by counting the number of classes he or she teaches each day. When you break it down this way, each class taught also receives an FTE value. For example:

If 1.0 FTE teaches five classes per day, each class equals .200 FTE.
If 1.0 FTE teaches six classes per day, each class equals .167 FTE.
If 1.0 FTE teaches seven classes per day, each class equals .142 FTE.

FTE May Refer to Both Positions and Individuals

An FTE value may be assigned to a *position* (band director) or an *individual* (Ms. Sanchez). That is, while Ms. Sanchez may be a full-time teacher (1.0 FTE), she may not necessarily work full time in just one curricular area (band director) because she may also have other duties (such as general music or study hall). The individual in table 8.1 teaches full time, but the music portion of the position equates to only .6 FTE (highlighted in *italics*).

Likewise, the position (band director) in the table is only .4 FTE. While the administration may perceive the district as having a full-time band director, it is the *individual* (Ms. Sanchez), not the *position* (band director), that is full time.

FTE Can Be Shared

Another common situation is revealed by the following two examples. Here you'll see how one 1.0 FTE elementary music position is shared by two individuals conducting classes at multiple schools. In table 8.2, both individuals are full time, but each position shares one-half of the elementary position. In table 8.3, the 1.0 FTE elementary position is shared by two part-

Table 8.1 Teacher Load (Based on 1.0 FTE as Five Classes per Day)

Period	Class	FTE
1	Computer Science	.2
2	*Concert Band*	.2
3	Study Hall	.2
4	*Varsity Band*	.2
5	*Music Appreciation*	.2

Table 8.2 Two Full-Time Teachers Sharing 1.0 FTE Elementary Position

Teacher 1 Assignment (1.0 FTE Contract)	FTE
Elementary Band (3 of 6 schools)	.5
Middle School Band	.5
Teacher 2 Assignment (1.0 FTE Contract)	FTE
Elementary Band (3 of 6 schools)	.5
High School Band	.5

Table 8.3   Two Part-Time Teachers Sharing 1.0 FTE Elementary Position

	FTE
Teacher 1 Assignment (.5 FTE Contract)	*FTE*
Elementary Band (3 of 6 schools)	.5
Teacher 2 Assignment (.5 FTE Contract)	*FTE*
Elementary Band (3 of 6 schools)	.5

time individuals. In both examples, the elementary music *position* equals 1.0 FTE.

A Board's-Eye View of Part-Time Teachers

Your school board's budget committee may see advantages to hiring part-time teachers, even though this may not always be in the best interest of music students or teachers. From the board's perspective, the reasons for hiring part-time teachers may be financial:

- Benefits may not be required for part-time instructors.
- Restrictions due to other budgetary decisions may exist.

Or practical:

- Student enrollment may not justify a full-time position.
- Some highly qualified teachers may be unable or unwilling to teach full time.

Here's How FTE Looks in a Real Budget

In a typical example, a district may assume it has thirty-seven full-time individuals teaching music. However, without doing a full analysis of FTE, the district may have little or no knowledge of the actual distribution of those positions among the various components of the music curriculum. Consequently, if the administration proposes cuts in one or more curricular areas it will be up to you to demonstrate the actual effect (loss) of FTE in each curricular area. While there are currently thirty-seven individuals on the music faculty in the school district example, actual load assignments only comprise a total of 36.24 FTE positions. This is demonstrated in table 8.4.

Asking the Right Questions Makes All the Difference

Are you asking some questions now that would simply not have occurred to you before? That's great! As you move through the rest of this section on FTE, you'll see more and more where—and how—you need to ask ques-

Table 8.4   FTE by Actual Position

Elementary General Music	10.67
Elementary Band	1.55
Elementary Orchestra	2.08
Elementary Choir	—
Middle School General Music	2.65
Middle School Band	3.37
Middle School Orchestra	3.38
Middle School Choir	4.11
High School General Music	—
High School Band	3.68
High School Orchestra	1.54
High School Choir	2.91
Nonmusic Assignments	.30
Travel Time	—
Music Coordinator/Supervisor	—
Total	36.24

Note: In this example, at least one individual was part time. Notice that no FTE is allocated to elementary choral music or coordination of the music curriculum. Some, but not all, individuals who work in multiple schools receive payment for travel time driving between schools; students lose instructional time, but the district had not factored in the loss of time in the classroom.

tions to evaluate just how much time a teacher actually spends on each area of the music curriculum. You'll begin to understand how your district's budget process works in relationship to the distribution of FTE.

Once you learn to ask the right questions—and understand how budgetary decisions impact students, teachers, and curricular offerings—then your role as a music advocate can really begin to have a positive impact!

ACTUAL FTE VALUE AND INDIVIDUAL STUDENT LOAD

Now that you have a basic concept of how FTE works, we'll look at how *actual FTE value* relates to an individual teacher's student load. You'll see, once again, why it's so important to use accurate, real numbers when analyzing what is needed for your school's music programs. Your district officials may be surprised to discover that your music program is a financial asset!

What Is Actual FTE Value?

The actual FTE value of each individual teacher is based upon the student load (or the actual number of students taught) of that instructor. Some teachers will have smaller loads than average, others larger (see the section on the fallacy of averages in this chapter). This often depends on the type of class being offered. For example, an advanced calculus class may have only fifteen students, while a typical music performance class may have fifty or more.

Actual FTE value is key to determining the economic viability of your school's music program. It is similar to the concept of the average FTE value, but is distinctly different because it is based on real numbers, not averages, estimates, or projections. The actual FTE value of an individual teacher is rarely (if ever) average.

How Is FTE Value Determined?

Your district first calculates the average student load based upon the total number of students divided by the total number of teachers, or the average class size multiplied by the number of classes taught. For example, if the average class size is determined to be twenty-five and each 1.0 FTE instructor teaches five classes, the average student load is determined to be 125.

But consider the example of a typical (1.0 FTE = 5 classes) secondary music teacher with an actual student load, as demonstrated in table 8.5.

Several observations may be made from the example of the student load illustrated in table 8.5.

- Students taking lessons or small ensembles may be non-load-bearing. That is, they are normally students who are pulled out from the other music or nonmusic classes who do not receive extra credit for their lessons. These cannot be counted as part of the music teacher's student load calculation.
- This teacher provides instruction for just four—not five—load-bearing classes. However, his student load (175) is fifty students higher than the average teacher's student load of 125 (five classes × twenty-five students).
- The *excess* student load of this teacher is equivalent to two classes of the average classroom teacher. This equates to an excess (above average)

Table 8.5   Student Load (1.0 FTE Band Teacher)

Class	Number of Students	FTE
Band 1	50	.2
Band 2	50	.2
Band 3	50	.2
Jazz Band	25	.2
Lessons/Ensembles	(Non-loadbearing)	.2
Totals	175	1.0 FTE

load of fifty students, or two extra classes and an excess value of .4 FTE. Therefore, this teacher has an FTE value of 1.4 classroom teachers. This higher student load (compared to the average student load of the classroom teacher) translates into a higher FTE value and much greater financial value provided to the district.

- While the teacher may have a 1.4 FTE value, he still only receives compensation equivalent to 1.0 FTE. The district uses the .4 FTE savings to fund other areas, primarily teachers with student loads (smaller classes) under the average figure.
- Since music performance teachers normally have a significantly higher FTE value than other classroom teachers, they carry the highest FTE value. This provides several benefits to the district:

  o It justifies any small-group or individual lessons provided to secondary students by the music teachers, even though they are not load bearing.
  o It justifies the inclusion of any music classes in the curriculum that may be under the normal minimum number of students required for a class.
  o It justifies the financial costs for an equivalent number of elementary music performance personnel.
  o It assists the district is maintaining smaller class sizes in other academic areas of the curriculum.

> Music performance teachers normally have larger student loads and higher FTE values—and that benefits your district.

As more than one superintendent has commented, "We are able to justify—and maintain—smaller classes in other academic areas because of the large classes in music. You don't save any money by cutting your music program."

Assuming your district does not have a music coordinator, the best advice I can give your music coalition is to have a statistics and finance committee, the local music coalition group that annually collects the kind of data requested on the music participation survey included in appendix A.

Once the survey data is collected, your committee should do the following.

1. Determine the student load of each music teacher;
2. Determine the average FTE value of all music performance teachers combined (band, choir, orchestra);

3. Compare the average FTE value of the music performance teachers to the average FTE figure used by your district.

My prediction? Your music program may actually be the most cost-effective program in the entire district!

How Average FTE Value Creates Budget Problems

By now you know how important it is to use accurate calculations of FTE when determining the number of teachers needed in each curricular area. If you pay close attention to another concept—average FTE value—you'll see how it is critical during the budget development process.

SCHOOLS DO NOT PROCESS BUDGETS LIKE BUSINESSES

First, your district budget is based on an estimate of all funds, or the anticipated revenue, available for staffing in your district. This revenue may include legislative initiatives, grants, and other monies that are not firmly in place during the budget development process. Unlike a business—which first establishes a vision (or intended profit margin) and then calculates how many products must be sold to meet that goal—your school district develops its budget based upon how much funding is anticipated. Your school board and administrators then use this estimate to determine how many staff positions may be added, maintained, or even cut. Your administration and board usually have a variety of contingency plans, each based on their most educated guesses as to what monies will eventually be provided.

Secondly, your district's budget development process related to staffing is based on the economic concept of average FTE value. The average FTE value or cost can vary widely between teaching and nonteaching staff.

Teaching versus Nonteaching Positions and Other Deciding Factors

The following formula is one commonly used to establish the average value of FTE in your school district:

The total dollar amount expended for faculty salaries and benefits, divided by the total number of faculty, determines the average cost (value) of 1.0 FTE faculty position.

The average dollar cost for nonteaching staff varies according to the average FTE value established for each job classification. For example:

- The average cost of 1.0 FTE teacher may be $50,000.
- The average cost for a 1.0 FTE administrator might be $75,000.
- The average cost for a 1.0 FTE clerical position may only be $25,000.

These figures may or may not include the cost of benefits, depending on the reporting practices of each district.

RATIO AVERAGES FACTOR INTO BUDGET DEVELOPMENT, TOO

Calculating the value of 1.0 FTE is also partially determined by ratios, which I will discuss in more detail later. For now, consider the importance of ratios as briefly outlined here.

- The student-faculty ratio (SFR, or average student load): the average number of students per each 1.0 FTE teaching position.
- The pupil-staff ratio (PSR): the average number of pupils or students per each 1.0 FTE position, including nonteaching staff as part of the staffing ratio.

The SFR and PSR are used to determine average class size or the number of students in the classroom during any single class session. The average class size will normally be larger than the PSR, and often larger than the SFR; how much larger depends on which nonteaching positions (such as guidance counselors, teaching assistants, or noncertified specialists) are included in the SFR.

Using Averages More Often Creates Problems, Not Solutions

The obvious problem with using a mathematical average as a budgetary yardstick is that averages do not provide a clear picture of the differences in cost or cost-benefit of specific programs or individual teaching positions. Add the sometimes shaky predictions of anticipated revenues to the equation, and you can see how using averages to make budgetary decisions may create a short-term financial crisis or, worse yet, long-term financial deficits.

Music performance teachers (band, choir, and orchestra) normally have a significantly higher FTE value than other teachers, because they have larger average student loads or SFRs. This gives them a higher FTE value than the average teacher, making their positions more valuable to maintain if the district is attempting to save money. *Music advocates who understand the difference between actual FTE value and average FTE value—and who use accurate calculations of FTE during budget development in their districts—say FTE is often the single most important tool they've used to save music programs.* It is the data needed to give credibility to the political power of their presence.

It provides a political "escape hatch" for school boards and administrators who desire to save music programs, while at the same time avoiding criticism for showing favoritism to special interest groups.

FTE: TEACHER SENIORITY AND THE FALLACY OF AVERAGES

School districts often attempt to solve a financial crisis by eliminating teaching positions. While on the surface this may seem to be the most equitable solution to a common and often complex problem, real numbers must be used—not averages—or the financial crisis will not really be averted.

Putting the Focus on Music Students

Several principles, some legal, must be taken into consideration.

- By law, eliminating the actual people (not positions) must be done according to seniority in the following order within any curricular area targeted for cuts: part time, nontenured, tenured.
- The district may be legally or contractually prevented from giving consideration to individual teacher quality or merit. However, the district may predetermine a goal for the number of cuts in any curricular area.
- *A financial crisis will always expose the education philosophy of your administration and board.* If your music teachers have not adequately demonstrated the curricular validity of music, a higher proportion of cuts may be aimed at the music program.
- Salaries of low-seniority teachers are normally below the average figure used by the school district in balancing the budget.
- If the district uses average FTE calculations during the budgetary process, the budget most likely will not be balanced because of the disparity between the average FTE cost used and the actual lower-than-average cost factor of the low-seniority individuals being cut.
- If the district wants to achieve the actual cost reduction designated it must base the budget upon actual salaries.
- As staff people are proposed for elimination, music program advocates must determine whether the district is using the average salary or the actual dollar amount for each person up for elimination.
- Cuts in the music program are normally listed by curricular area, so cuts may significantly affect the quality of student instruction. For example, a low-seniority high school orchestra teacher may be replaced by a high-seniority elementary general music teacher, even though the latter may never have had any educational preparation or experience to teach strings.

A Closer Look at the Numbers and Seniority

So let's say your school district has come up with a proposal to solve an impending financial crisis. They announce the elimination of 5.2 FTE positions (held by low-seniority instrumental music teachers). By using the average teacher salary figure of $25,232, the district claims this will produce a savings of $196,810.

Sounds like the crisis is solved (even though we, of course, don't like the fact that it takes a serious chunk out of the music program), doesn't it? However, with the cooperation of all the music teachers in the district, advocates compile the data in table 8.6, demonstrating the salaries of the instrumental music teachers organized according to seniority order.

The 5.2 FTE low-seniority positions (eight individuals) proposed for elimination were in elementary band (D, E, F, G), secondary band (G, H), and orchestra (D, E). Table 8.7 indicates the financial savings when advocates added up the salaries of the lowest seniority 5.2 FTE teachers slated for elimination.

As you can see, the district would only save $131,206, a budgetary miscalculation of over $65,606. To actually save the anticipated amount of $196,810, the district would have needed to eliminate 7.8 positions, an action they publicly declared they would not take. (The first part of the victory—saving 2.6 FTE.)

Playing by the *Real* Numbers: It's the Only Way to Go

Thanks to the legwork of music program advocates, this district was forced to go back to the drawing board, so to speak, with calculators in hand. They came up with a solution to the financial crisis that was based on actual figures, not averages.

Table 8.6   Instrumental Music Teacher Salaries (in High to Low Seniority Order)

Elementary Band		Secondary Band		Orchestra	
Teacher	Salary	Teacher	Salary	Teacher	Salary
A	$59,335	A	$61,148	A	$56,334
B	57,582	B	59,334	B	42,254
C	56,443	C	57,583	C	30,783
D	30,408	D	57,582	D	29,634
E*	10,990	E	42,636	E	22,286
F*	10,296	F	33,086		
G*	6,236	G*	17,370		
		H*	3,986		

*Part-time positions

Table 8.7   Instrumental Music Teacher Salaries (5.2 FTE Lowest Seniority Positions)

Elementary Band		*$57,930*
Teacher D	$30,408	
*Teacher E	10,990	
*Teacher F	10,296	
*Teacher G	6,236	
Secondary Band		*21,356*
*Teacher G	17,370	
*Teacher H	3,986	
Orchestra		*51,920*
Teacher D	29,634	
Teacher E	22,286	
Total		*131,206*

*Part-time positions

In this district, when advocates exposed the fallacy of the administration's average calculations, the public saw tangible proof that undermined the credibility of the budgetary decision-making process they had perhaps blindly trusted. This provided a strong foundation for the advocates' case that actual figures were necessary and, better yet, it helped advocates when it came time to demonstrate the financial viability of the music curriculum.

Using all of these calculations, along with other information related to student participation in music programs and the FTE student load advantage of music performance teachers, the district was able to save its entire music curriculum.

FTE and the Danger of Using Averages

I have come to believe the concept of *average* places a school district in greater financial jeopardy than any other factor. The reason? Averages, as an economist friend of mine likes to say, "are theoretical numbers that don't exist in reality. Statisticians use them to reduce a large amount of information to a single number, one that means much less than they presume."

Or, to put it another way, the average daily high temperature in Minneapolis is 45 degrees. As any Minnesotan will tell you, this average temperature means very little in the month of January or in July.

Why Do School Administrators Use Averages?

It is difficult to fault a local school administration or board for using averages during the standard budgetary process. Your district establishes several average figures to help calculate their annual costs. Administrators often use several average calculations applied to various line items or broad budget-

ary categories, because averages can be a useful estimating tool to help calculate costs. The danger lies in using them without crunching them up
against actual hard numbers.

School districts tend to over-rely on averages for a couple of reasons, even
though using averages goes against many basic principles of accounting or
good business management. First of all, the typical district finance department is far understaffed. This means it's difficult, if not nearly impossible,
to allocate precious staff time to calculate such detailed information as the
FTE value of each program or teacher. As you know, calculations of FTE
value are based on research and careful data collection; and then that raw
information must be analyzed to create a realistic picture of your district's
budgetary needs and assets. This takes a fair amount of staff (or board finance committee) time and a commitment to accuracy. Many districts are
not able—or willing—to allocate their resources to this task.

The second—and far more damaging—reason why school districts rely
on averages is that educational systems tend to be driven by the philosophies and opinions of the decision makers. Using this approach is the opposite of making sound decisions by examining and evaluating the financial and accounting realities.

Averages Don't Make Good Business—or Educational—Sense

Can you imagine any business assuming that all its salespeople earn the
same average salary and produce the same average amount of sales? Or can
you imagine any business cutting the lowest seniority sales staff—regardless
of the productivity level or financial value of that individual?

If the business used such a process, it would soon be bankrupt.

When a school district is in financial crisis, its educational philosophy is
often very clearly exposed. For example, if administrators assume all teachers have the same average cost (or salary), they may propose cuts in curricular areas they see as educationally least important. Using a system based on
average financial calculations ignores the cost-benefit ratio of specific programs and exposes the educational philosophy of the leadership.

When cuts are based on educational philosophy or opinions (or even just
simply "gut feelings") about which curricular areas are most or least important—or when the elimination of teachers is based on seniority (usually
required by contract or law)—this type of decision making ignores the
value of maintaining those programs.

Averages Don't Solve Problems—They Create Them!

Using averages ignores the fact that the teachers with the highest FTE value
are often those with the lowest salaries and often also the highest student

loads. Music performance teachers often fall into this category.

When administrators or school board members rely on averages to structure their budget process, they often create financially problematic scenarios such as the ones listed below.

- If the district eliminates a music performance position or program with a high FTE value, they must compensate by increasing class sizes by a greater amount than if they eliminated a position or program with lesser FTE value.
- If the district eliminates a music position or program (or any part of a program) that causes a reduction in student enrollment in those programs with the highest FTE value, the district will then need to hire additional classroom teachers with lower FTE values to replace these high FTE value teachers.
- If the district eliminates teachers with lower seniority, they will be eliminating positions with lower FTE value. Therefore, additional positions will need to be cut to equal the anticipated budgetary savings projected by using the average FTE value.

Districts innately understand this, of course. But, in the presence of a financial crisis, decision makers may be swayed by proposals to cut programs and staff because they appear to make sense or be easier—on the surface. That is, they may decide to go with their "gut feelings" about which programs have higher value as curricular entities instead of taking the time to analyze carefully the financial impact of their proposed cuts.

What Can You Do to Counteract the Use of Averages?

The use of averages points out yet another reason why music advocates need to be involved in the budgetary process. As well-informed advocates—advocates who understand how to calculate FTE values and also know how to develop and present impact statements detailing the damaging effects of proposed cuts—we have the opportunity (and the responsibility) to insist that decisions are *not* based on averages. We need the hard, concrete data to support our proposals—and to show decision makers why it's not a good idea to rely on averages.

As you present your reasons why averages are damaging to the music program, you must clearly demonstrate the fiscal viability of the music program, using impact statements based on accurate research and calculations that include a clear analysis of the FTE value of teachers and programs. You must show there's absolutely nothing average about your music program—using dollars, cents, *and* business sense!

FTE AND STAFFING (A CASE STUDY)

How to Save a Music Program (Even If a Staff Position Is Eliminated)

I received an urgent telephone call from a band director late one evening and the conversation went something like this.

"Our district is going through a budget crisis. The administration published a list of cuts. None of the music programs were on the list, so I went personally and checked with the superintendent. I was told the entire elementary band program was being eliminated, primarily because of the recommendation of the elementary band teacher. What can we do to save the elementary band program?"

As we talked, I realized the district planned to eliminate the elementary band position under a hidden cut, or one that didn't specifically include the word "music." It appeared in the administrative budget document as "Eliminate 1.0 FTE Elementary Position."

I also learned that some personal issues had clouded the decision-making process.

Before we get into this particular situation, please remember that FTE can be used to refer to both programs (elementary band) and positions (band teacher). Understanding the distinction between the two makes all the difference in the world to students eager to participate in music making.

Analyzing this situation, you can see how things actually worked out to benefit the students who wanted to be in the elementary school band.

The elementary band teacher (teacher 5 in table 8.8) was a personal friend of the superintendent. She had been granted the position despite the unanimous protest of the (all-male) band staff. Since hiring of teacher 5, nearly 90 percent of students enrolled in elementary band had dropped out. This teacher's recommendation to eliminate the program was an act of revenge against the other band instructors.

As a music advocate trying to save this elementary band program, the first and most important step was to find out how teachers are spending their time each day. That's where the music participation survey (see appendix A) came into play.

When the teachers completed the music participation survey, some very interesting and significant data was revealed. Careful analysis of the data led to a relatively easy solution in which everyone came out as a winner. By analyzing the FTE as it relates to both positions and programs, the elementary band curriculum was saved.

Look Closely at These Actual FTE Numbers

The class load for each of the 5.0 FTE band instructors is listed in table 8.8. One full-time teaching position, teacher 5, was targeted by the administration for elimination. But if this elementary band teaching position was eliminated, how could this elementary band program possibly be saved?

The proposal called for the elimination of 1.0 FTE position specified as teacher 5 (the elementary band position). On the surface, since there were five full-time teachers, it seemed reasonable to assume that each teacher represented 20 percent of the band staff. However, upon further examination, it became clear that teachers 1–4 were not teaching band 100 percent of their time. The proportion of FTE each of them spent on study hall, lunchroom supervision, and non-band teaching assignments reduced the amount of FTE allocated to actual staffing of the band program. This is demonstrated in table 8.9.

Table 8.8   Band Teacher FTE

School	Class	Enrollment	FTE
Band Teacher #1 (1.0 FTE)			
High School	Band/Lessons	115	.8
High School	Hall Supervisions		.2
Band Teacher #2 (1.0 FTE)			
High School	Band/Lessons	(See Teacher #1)	.4
High School	Music Theory	13	.2
High School	Choir Acc.		.2
High School	Study Hall		.2
Band Teacher #3 (1.0 FTE)			
Middle School #1	Grade 6 Band	48	.3
Middle School #1	Grades 7–8 Band	75	.3
Middle School #1	Hall/Lunch Super		.4
Band Teacher #4 (1.0 FTE)			
Middle School #2	Grade 6 Band	46	.3
Middle School #2	Grade 7–8 Band	64	.3
Middle School #2	Hall/Lunch Super		.4
Band Teacher #5 (1.0 FTE)			
Elementary 1–9	Grade 5 Band	263	1.0

Table 8.9   Band Director Teaching Assignments (Non-band FTE)

Teacher	Class	FTE
Teacher #1	HS Study Hall	.2
Teacher #2	HS Study Hall	.2
	Music Theory	.2
	Choir Accompanist	.2
Teacher #3	MS Study Hall/Lunch	.4
Teacher #4	MS Study Hall/Lunch	.4
Total non-band FTE		1.6

The Solution Is in the Numbers

In this situation, the district assumed that five full-time positions (5.0 FTE) were dedicated to band instruction. But in reality, if you subtract the 1.6 FTE non-band assignments from the total 5.0 FTE teaching positions, the district actually had only 3.4 FTE band positions. This meant that eliminating a 1.0 FTE teaching position reduced the available time to teach band by nearly 30 percent, *not* just 20 percent (or one of five teachers) as might appear to be true with only a surface analysis. Further, as an advocate of music education programs for young people, it was totally unjustifiable from either a philosophical or financial perspective to assign 1.2 FTE of the load of teachers 1–4 to study hall or lunchroom supervision.

By working together and keeping the needs of the elementary school band students foremost in mind, music education advocates and the district used *real* numbers to avert the crisis.

Here's what happened. The band directors agreed to accept the cut of 1.0 FTE position if the nonmusic responsibilities were removed from their loads. They would assume teaching responsibilities for continuing the grade 5 band program with the FTE formerly used to provide lunch and hall supervision.

- The elementary band program was saved for the students and the district was able to resolve the budget crisis.
- The district converted all study hall and lunchroom supervision (the equivalent of 1.2 FTE) from teachers 1–4 to elementary band instruction. This redistribution allowed the district to save the elementary band program by having teachers 1–4 share the teaching of band in nine elementary schools, and there was a net .2 FTE gain in band staffing.
- The district was still able to eliminate 1.0 FTE position. Teacher 5 was allowed to maintain a non-band position within the district by going back to a regular teaching position. This teacher was no longer able to negatively affect students interested in elementary band.

- Four dedicated and effective music teachers now spent their time teaching band, not supervising study hall or lunchroom.

FTE and the Staffing Ratio

Your school district uses several related financial values—FTE, SFR, and PSR—to establish the number of students assigned to each classroom teacher. As you might already guess, these calculations form the basis of many important budget decisions that directly affect the strength of your school's music curriculum.

What Is the Staffing Ratio and How Is It Used?

The staffing ratio is based on the relationship between two basic figures—the number of pupil units and the number of FTE staff positions (teaching and nonteaching). The staffing ratio is used to determine the amount of funding available for hiring (or retaining or cutting) staff.

The pupil unit (PU) is the equivalent of one full-time student (or 1.0 FTE PU). Your district defines PUs by calculating the number of courses taken per day, week, or year. It's important to understand that the PU number is not necessarily the same as the number of students in a grade, classroom, or school. For example, if kindergarten students attend school for only one-half of each day, each student is the equivalent of .5 PU.

If there is a staffing ratio of 28:1 at your school, your local school will receive a budgetary allocation equivalent to the average cost of 1.0 FTE staff position for every 28.0 PU.

How the Staffing Ratio Is Determined

You can quickly see, then, that changes in enrollment may have a direct affect on the number of teachers employed in each school. Other factors also affect the total budget for staff, including whether FTE positions are exclusively for teachers, or whether they include nonteaching staff as well.

The staffing ratio is established by your school district's central administration and approved by the school board. Once defined, the staffing ratio offers guidance to each school's site administrator (or principal) regarding how funds may be allocated for staff and teaching positions. The staffing ratio provided to your local school is based upon your school board's particular definition of SFR or PSR.

Generally speaking, the SFR is the *average number of students for each teacher*. It is calculated by simply dividing the number of PU by the number of teacher FTE. Some districts may also include nonteaching staff, such as guidance counselors, in the SFR.

The PSR is used to determine overall staffing needs based on the number of pupils in the district. This ratio is the number of students per each 1.0 FTE position (and may, at the discretion of the school board, include all staff as defined by the district).

Since the salaries of administrators, teachers, and clerical and other staff may vary widely, districts often assign different average values to the 1.0 FTE in each of the various categories of staffing during budgetary planning sessions.

Local Discretionary Decisions May Affect the Staffing Ratio

The staffing ratio directly relates to class size, of course, but it is primarily used by the various levels of administration to determine the amount of funding available for staff hires. Unless specifically defined by the school district, site administrators normally have autonomous discretion in the expenditure of funds designated for staffing. In other words, the extent to which a principal chooses to use staffing funds for nonteaching positions will proportionately increase the average class size and decrease the number of teaching positions.

The staffing ratio may be consistently used throughout all of your school district, or it may be individually calculated by grade or curricular area. For example, the staffing ratio may vary according to grade level as determined by district philosophy and demonstrated in table 8.10.

If we assume from the example in table 8.10 that the average 1.0 staff FTE equals $50,000, and that there are 1,000 students in grades 4–6, we can assume that the site administrator will receive funding equal to 40 FTE or $2,000,000, as shown below.

1. The staffing ratio in grades 4–6 is 25:1.
2. One thousand total students divided by the PU figure of 25 results in 40 FTE.
3. Forty FTE times the average FTE value of $50,000 equals a budget allocation of $2,000,000.
4. The site administrator then hires staff according to needs as determined autonomously, by district guidelines, or in collaboration with other staff, teachers, and/or the community.

Table 8.10   District Staffing Ratio Example

Grade	Staffing Ratio
K–3	24:1 (1.0 FTE per 24 PU)
4–6	25:1 (1.0 FTE per 25 PU)
7–9	26:1 (1.0 FTE per 26 PU)
10–12	26.5:1 (1.0 FTE per 26.5 PU)

The Staffing Ratio's Impact on Music Teachers

Music teachers may—or, in some cases, may not—be a part of these staffing formulas. Here are some important cautions and considerations:

- Elementary general music teachers are often excluded from the staffing formula. This is because they may be interpreted as a part of the central administrative budget for providing preparatory time for classroom teachers, or assigned to multiple schools. If this is the case in your school district, this budget item should be considered part of the elementary staffing formula, not part of the music budget.
- Elementary instrumental music teachers or other itinerants (i.e., teachers with multiple school assignments) are often excluded from the staffing formula. This may happen when management of their salary line items fall under the central (as opposed to site) administration and may be based upon the size of the school population.
- Secondary music teachers are normally part of the regular staffing formula.
- Staffing FTE provided for persons serving as chair, coordinator, or supervisor of the music curriculum may or may not be funded with the staffing formula.

District Financial Status and Ratio Point

Finally, one more crucial aspect of the staffing ratio must be considered: the overall financial health of your school district. The staffing ratio may be altered—in some cases quite significantly—due to increasing costs and reductions in available funding. One indicator that the staffing ratio may be altered (either by new hires or staffing reductions) is use of the key phrase "changes in class size."

Remember, school administrators use the staffing ratio to determine the amount of funding available for new staff hires. If the ratio of PU to FTE teachers in grades 4–6 in the example is changed from 25:1 (1.0 staff FTE per 25 PU) to 26:1 (1.0 staff FTE per 26 PU), several financial changes occur:

1. The site administrator will have a reduction in funding.
2. The site administrator (as per staffing ratios—see table 8.10) will assign only 1.0 FTE for each 26 students, and will therefore have approximately 38 FTE (a reduction of 2.0 FTE).
3. The site administrator will then have to make staffing cuts in either teaching or nonteaching positions—or both—to recover the deficit.

Changes to the staffing ratio are expressed in the form of a *ratio point* and assigned a financial value by the district. The cost of a ratio point is the financial value associated with changing the PU in the ratio formula by 1.0 PU. Dealing with cost reductions by changing the ratio point makes it possible for the district to maintain all curricular options *if it so chooses*.

Once again, you can see how crucial it is that music advocates remain well informed and active throughout the entire school budget development process. Armed with accurate information and a solid working knowledge of how staffing ratios are used to establish the budget for music programs, advocates can have a positive impact on expanding and protecting music participation for all students.

Every true music educator believes that every child should have the opportunity to participate in music, and music should be a part of every child's basic (core) education. Unfortunately, the success of any music program is rarely measured by achieving those goals. Success is more likely determined by less reliable means, such as the size of a single performing group (band, orchestra, or choir) or the number of awards school groups have received. This type of success, though certainly meaningful, often has little or nothing to do with whether there is adequate staffing for student music programs.

The situation is complicated by at least two additional factors:

1. The teaching loads of current music staff may already be so large they cannot possibly teach a greater number of students.
2. The community, school board members, administration, and even music teachers may hold an underlying elitist attitude that music is only for a few truly gifted or talented students. As stated earlier, one music coordinator stated, "We start 500 grade 5 students in instrumental music each year and, by the time they are in high school, we have them weeded down to the best fifty!"

So, how can proactive music education advocates use data related to the staffing ratio (SFR) in music to address these problems? Real data makes it possible to document some of the underlying issues that can limit student access to quality music programming.

SFR Data: Four Valuable Discoveries

Here are four of the most common positive outcomes that may be achieved by data collection and analysis:

1. Data can reveal the relationship between the SFR established in the district budgeting process and the (usually higher) SFR of music teachers.
2. Data can show that it's possible for every child to receive a music education based on the relative adequacy of staffing.

3. Data can demonstrate program growth, that is, the need to add more positions to provide instruction to the greatest number of students.
4. Data can demonstrate the negative impact that proposed staff cuts would have on students' ability to receive a music education.

SFR Data: Revealing the Problems

Look carefully at tables 8.11, 8.12, and 8.13. Each table shows data samples about current staffing in a school district's music program. And, as you'll see, whether the district is small or large, each reveals a lack of awareness about how many staff are really needed to provide a semblance of excellence in music programming.

Table 8.11 represents the average allocation of FTE teachers per school in each area of the music curriculum.

People in the community and district generally believed that the music program was healthy. This was based primarily on wonderful media coverage about the achievements of selected performing groups within the district. But look closely at the data and you'll see quite a different picture. Here are just a few key observations about the data extracted from table 8.11.

- There were no general music instructors at the elementary level. (Note: Those positions had been eliminated in a previous round of cuts.)
- If you divide 29 elementary schools by 3 FTE teachers, each instrumental music teacher provided instruction to students in grades 5 and 6 in at least nine schools.

Table 8.11   Music Faculty: Average FTE Available per School by Area of Instruction

Music Teacher Category	Number of Schools	Total FTE Available	Average FTE per School
Elementary General Music	29	0.000	0.000
Elementary Band	29	3.000	0.103
Elementary Orchestra	29	3.000	0.103
Middle School General Music	6	0.333	0.067
Middle School Band	6	2.167	0.361
Middle School Orchestra	6	1.332	0.222
Middle School Choir	6	1.834	0.306
High School General Music	4	1.000	0.250
High School Band	4	3.000	0.750
High School Orchestra	4	0.800	0.200
High School Choir	4	2.100	0.525

Table 8.12   SFR by Area of Instruction: Large District (Based on the Number of Students Eligible)

SFR Category	SFR
All students (K–12) to all music faculty	1699:1
Eligible elementary students to instrumental music faculty	879:1
All secondary students to all music faculty	1162:1
Eligible secondary students to general music faculty	10953:1
Eligible secondary students to band faculty	2826:1
Eligible secondary students to orchestra faculty	6848:1
Eligible secondary students to choir faculty	3711:1

Table 8.13   SFR by Area of Instruction: Small District (Based on the Number of Public School Students Eligible)

SFR Category	SFR
All students (K–12) to all music faculty	419:1
All secondary students to secondary music faculty	430:1
Eligible secondary students to band faculty	602:1
Eligible secondary students to choir faculty	2258:1

- If you add all the available FTE for music instruction at the middle schools, you arrive at a total of 5.666. When you divide that number by 6 schools, you have less than 1.0 FTE per school for general music, band, choir, *and* orchestra.
- Statistically, no school in the district had a full-time instructor in any area of the music curriculum; that is, all teachers appeared to have multiple school assignments.

Bottom line? The lack of adequate staffing in any curricular area rendered it impossible to provide adequate music instruction to the greatest student population.

This problem is further demonstrated in table 8.12, which illustrates the SFR of music teachers in a large district. The SFR is calculated by comparing the number of students eligible to participate in each curricular area in music to the available number of FTE teachers actually providing instruction in each area. Similar results are observed from statistical data collected in a small district with only one public school at each level, as shown in table 8.13. While minimal FTE was allocated for elementary general music, none was provided for elementary band, choir, or orchestra.

The evidence is clear in both large and small districts: With such high SFR levels it is simply not possible for every child to participate in music in any area of the K–12 music curriculum. Previous cuts in staffing may be part of the problem. Additional cuts would only make the situation worse. The only solution is to assign new FTE to the music curriculum, that is, add music staffing.

REVERSE ECONOMICS:
DEVELOPING A FISCAL CASE FOR THE MUSIC PROGRAM

The major factor in developing a fiscal case for the music program lies in the fact that the music performance classes are curricular, that is, they are held during the regular school day. Most people do not understand that money is not saved by cutting music programs, but by making them stronger. Herein lies the concept of reverse economics: the long-term effects of the elimination of a program are more costly than the initial savings anticipated. The economic ramifications of low enrollment or the loss of student participation in the music performance program are significant. There are three principles here.

1. If the average (district-wide) student loads of secondary music performance teachers *are smaller than* those of classroom teachers, you will be in the weakest financial position to preserve or build your program. If this is the case, you must ask why. The answers to the "why" question often provide the solution saving the program. For example, you may be able to point out administrative issues that prevent student participation such as guidance counselors who tell students not to take the arts, or a refusal to schedule music performance classes in a way that facilitates student participation, or the impact of previous cuts to the program (particularly at the elementary level).
2. Second, if the average student loads of secondary music performance teachers *are the same* as those of other classroom teachers, you are financially justified in fighting to take only your fair share of cuts. Political expediency may seem to indicate that you accept equal or some cuts if for no other reason than being able to be the first to ask for program reinstatement as funds become available in the future. *However, it is strongly recommended that music supervisors, music teachers, and advocate assume a posture of no cuts or it will appear that you are suggesting them.* In this case the administration and school board will be able to blame you for any cuts which are made, and you may be less likely to get them back.
3. Finally, it may be that the average student loads of secondary music performance teachers *are normally larger* than those of the regular classroom teachers, and this is where music programs should be economically most secure. Any cuts in music programs under these circumstances are

economically counterproductive. The primary cost factor in education is personnel (see discussion of FTE and FTE value earlier in the chapter). The most cost-efficient personnel are those who provide instruction to the largest number of students in a given class period or who carry the largest student loads.

This financial significance of facilitating high participation in music performance courses may be demonstrated through analysis of the data collected in the public school music participation survey (see appendix A). (Note: The data contained in table 8.14 have been reduced to include only band enrollments to simplify the information. Normally, all music performing organizations would be included in the data to provide more complete information.)

In the case shown in table 8.14 the district proposed the elimination of grade 5 band. Observations from the profile of student enrollment in band included the following factors.

- The district consisted of ten elementary schools, two junior high schools, one high school, and an alternative high school.
- Students enrolled at elementary school I and in the alternative high school were not offered the option to participate in band. It would be possible to make an equal access case in this circumstance.
- Student enrollments in band are listed by school and grade, with 1,104 student participants.
- District enrollments are indicated by grade, with 5,621 students in grades 5–12 eligible for participation.
- A total of 585 (load-bearing/non-pull-out) students participate in band in the secondary grades 7–12.
- The percentage of eligible students participating in band is indicated by grade, with 20 percent of all eligible students participating.
- Enrollment disparities were evident in individual schools and between grades district wide. These should be examined for causation. (Districts identified as of qualitative excellence (Culver, 1990) consider 65 percent of grade 5 students as a minimum target level for participation in instrumental music, and a maximum of 15 percent attrition between any two grades.)
- If enrollment disparities (as related to attrition) were reduced to a minimum of 15 percent in all grades, student participation would increase to 1,310. Of particular significance are the percentages in grades 6, 7, 8, 9, and 11.
- If the district achieved the quantitative status of a profile of excellence, that is, 65 percent in instrumental music (including orchestra) there would be 1,923 students participating in band (and orchestra).

Table 8.14 Student Participation: Band

School	Gr 5	Gr 6	Gr 7	Gr 8	Gr 9	Gr 10	Gr 11	Gr 12	Total
Elementary A	30	10							40
Elementary B	38	25							63
Elementary C	38	40							78
Elementary D	46	48							94
Elementary E	7	12							19
Elementary F	25	20							45
Elementary G	33	45							78
Elementary H	38	32							70
Elementary I									0
Elementary J	15	17							32
Junior High A			98	62	41				201
Junior High B			53	53	47				153
High School						107	64	60	231
Alternative HS									0
Band Totals	270	249	151	115	88	107	64	60	1104
District Enrollment by grade	610	639	685	696	787	769	732	703	5621
Percent of District Enrollment	44%	39%	22%	17%	11%	14%	9%	9%	20%
Enrollment Disparity		-8%	-39%	-24%	-23%	22%	-40%	-6%	
Maximum Disparity 15%	270	230	195	166	141	120	102	87	1310
65% Grade 5, 15% maximum attrition	397	337	286	244	207	176	150	127	1923
Eliminate Grade 5	0	87	53	40	31	37	22	21	292

- Based on national case studies of the anticipated long-term 65 percent loss of students due to the proposed elimination of grade 5 band, within just a few years only 292 students would remain in the band program. This is a loss of 1,108 students.

If we combine the band, choir, and orchestra enrollment data for the same district, and the FTE information gathered from pages 1–3 of the public school music participation survey, we can determine the average FTE value of the music performance teachers. This is summarized in table 8.15, based on the following information.

- There were 2,589 students in band, choir, and orchestra in all grades.
- There were 1,516 secondary band, choir, and orchestra students.
- There were 10.2 FTE secondary band, choir, and orchestra teachers.

- The average student load of the secondary music performance teacher was 149 (1,516 students/10.2 FTE teachers).
- The average student load of the secondary nonmusic classroom teacher was 116 (5 classes × 23.2 students) (Note: The average student load of nonmusic classroom teachers was inflated by the large music performance classes.)

Based on the comparison of student loads of music performance and nonmusic classroom teachers illustrated in table 8.15, the following factors became evident.

- There were 10.2 FTE positions assigned to the grades 5–12 band, choir, and orchestra curriculum.
- The average student load of the secondary music performance teacher equated to 1.4 FTE value as compared to nonmusic classroom teachers.
- The 10.2 FTE secondary music performance teachers total FTE value was equivalent to 14.28 FTE nonmusic classroom teachers, an excess of 4.08 FTE. Therefore, it could be demonstrated that this overload:

    o Included the costs for any small-group or individual lessons provided to secondary students by the music teachers.
    o Justified the inclusion of any music classes in the curriculum that were under the normal minimum number required to offer a class.
    o Assisted the district in maintaining smaller class sizes in other academic areas of the curriculum.
    o Paid for the elementary feeder program equivalent to the excess 4.08 FTE value.

While districts may target smaller music classes at the secondary level for elimination, they rarely recommend the elimination of secondary music

Table 8.15   Average Student Loads (Secondary Example)

FTE	Classification	Classes x Students	Student Load
1.0	Nonmusic Classroom Teacher	5 x 23.2	116
1.0	Band, Choir, Orchestra Teacher	5 x 29.8	149
2.0	Teachers		265
1.0	Nonmusic Classroom Teacher	5 x 23.2	116
1.0	Nonmusic Classroom Teacher (new)	5 x 23.2	116
.4	New Classroom Teacher (new)	2 x 16.5	33
2.4			265

performance (band, choir, orchestra) classes, because they recognize the value of these large class sizes. Normally they initially eliminate the elementary feeder system because of its nature as a "pull-out" program. This is because they make the assumption that there is already a classroom teacher to manage the students, and that there will be no long-term negative effect on the secondary enrollment in band.

However, extensive national case studies indicate that when initial participation in an instrumental and/or choral feeder system is delayed until grade 6 or later, the subsequent decline in student participation at the secondary level will be a minimum of 65 percent. Within four years this decline in participation is incurred at the high school. Several reasons appear to be the cause of the decline in student participation.

- The "window of learning" closes between the ages of ten and eleven. Students are not as apt to participate if the starting date is delayed until grade 6 or later.
- Elementary students who enroll in instrumental music who have had one or two years experience will be required to drop the program until they reach a later grade. They are not likely to start over again. (For example, if a district eliminated an elementary instrumental music program in grades 4–6, students in grades 4 and 5 would not be able to participate again until grade 7.)
- Students are less likely to begin study of a music instrument in grades 6 or 7 because of the increasing number of other competing opportunities.
- Students who are not allowed to begin participation in music performance until grades 6 or 7 are less patient with the rate of progress in skill development and are more likely to drop out of the program than those who begin study in grade 5.
- The normal high for attrition rates are when students change schools (levels). They are less apt to enroll in new areas of academic pursuit if the start of a new program coincides with a change in school sites.
- The elimination of the elementary feeder will cause a decline in morale at the secondary levels, spawning an increase in attrition rates.
- Elimination of teaching positions in music normally causes a major change in teaching assignments. Combined with other factors, an unexpected change in instructors becomes an additional deterrent to continued participation.

Therefore, any circumstance that causes a decline in student enrollment or prevents students from participation will have a negative cost effect on the district budget. In the example above, the anticipated long-term loss of 931 secondary band students (caused by the proposed elimination of grade

5 band) would necessitate the eventual employment of 8.0 FTE secondary nonmusic classroom teachers (931 students/116 student load average), while maintaining an appropriate number of music performance FTE to continue the program of those students still electing participation.

The elimination of an elementary music performance "pull-out" program only delays the reverse economic effect for a year or two until those (former or potential) students reach the secondary school level.

A second case study illustrates the financial effect. In this district the administrative proposal was to eliminate 70 percent of the orchestra staff and 48 percent of the band staff. Initially this would have equated to 7.8 FTE. However, the district indicated that they would only cut 5.2 FTE band and orchestra positions for an anticipated annual savings of $156,000. (A quick calculation and you can see that they were using an average salary figure of $30,000, excluding benefits.) What they had not done is calculate the impact on student enrollment. In figure 8.1 you will note that there were 2,529 students in band and orchestra in grades 4–12, including two high schools, four middle schools, and eight elementary schools.

In the first year of cuts as proposed approximately 1,800 instrumental students in grades 4, 5, and 6 would have been eliminated from participation in band and orchestra. No new students would be started in either program until they reached grade 7. In addition, enough middle school students would have been eliminated so that the district would have needed to open twenty-nine new classes and hire 6.4 FTE classroom teachers to replace the 5.2 FTE instrumental teachers to teach former instrumental music students, at a cost of $192,000.

By year three, with no new students having been started during the intervening years, more non-instrumental students moving into the upper grades, and an equivalent number of senior classes having graduated, the district would be required to hire 10.2 cumulative FTE for fifty classes at a cost of $300,000. Only 360 combined band and orchestra students would have remained in the program for the fourteen schools. The parents suggested eliminating the instrumental music program totally in one of the two high schools in the district and its feeder schools, so that at least one school cluster in the district would have a complete instrumental music curriculum with adequate staffing. (Some districts do this and call it a magnet school.)

By year five, for all practical purposes the program would have collapsed. The district would have needed to hire 12.6 cumulative classroom FTE for sixty-three classes for former instrumental music students at a cost of $378,000. Added to the anticipated savings of $156,000 this would have amounted to an annual budget miscalculation (reverse economic effect) of $534,000. The board overruled the administrative proposal and reinstated all of the instrumental music positions.

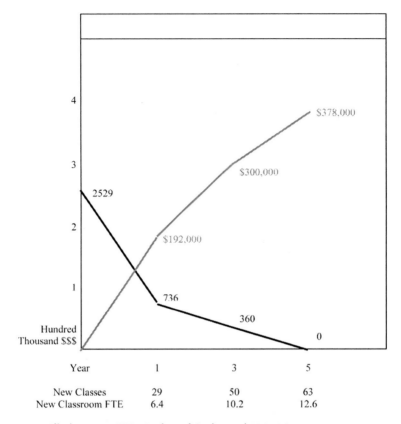

Figure 8.1   Eliminate 5.2 FTE: Projected Savings—$156,000

> "As you learn the concept of reverse economics you will come to
> understand that money is not saved by cutting music programs."
> —Burton M. Nygren, superintendent
> (*The Instrumentalist,* August 1991, 18)
>
> * * *
>
> A financial crisis always exposes the underlying educational
> philosophy of your school district.

"PAY-TO-PLAY": PARTICIPATION FEES

One of the common techniques used to offset budgetary shortfalls, particularly in the area of extracurricular activities, is to assess participation fees. At
the basic level this is simply a convenient means of increasing the level of

taxation for those who can afford or choose to have their children participate. The primary way to avoid "pay-to-play" for participation in music is
to carefully define the different aspects of the music program to avoid having them categorized as extracurricular (see discussion of curricular, cocurricular, and extracurricular programs in chapter 4).

Several other observations or considerations should also be made related
to the adoption of participation or instrument rental fees.

- Adoption of participation fees can lead to significant attrition, particularly in areas of economic stress.
- Parents and students already provide significant subsidy to the district
  by purchasing and maintaining their own instruments.
- Parents and students may be asked to pay a uniform fee. This fee is
  intended in part to provide for new uniforms.
- Students who use school-owned instruments often are asked pay a
  rental fee for usage.
- Parents and students may already provide extensive subsidy to the
  school district with current fund-raising activities.
- It is often unclear what actual revenues and expenditures are used to
  determine the perceived costs of extracurricular programs (salary stipends, uniforms, travel, capital expense, etc.).

Of greater significance is the apparent inequity of adding another fee to
these students as demonstrated in the following two case studies.

Case Study: West High School

In the case of West High School, the administration calculated the net
Board of Education cost of twenty-four programs identified by the district
budget as extracurricular. The board and administration were provided with
the data in table 8.16 to justify the addition of participation fees.

The most obvious factor missing from the information is the failure to
demonstrate the cost per pupil. This is another illustration of an adult-
centered decision-making process. The attempt was to balance the budget,
and the impact on the individual student or program was not taken into
consideration. On the surface it seemed obvious that the music program, in
particular band, was very expensive, as indicated below.

- Of the twenty-four categories, band ranked number 5 in net Board of
  Education (BOE) cost.
- Of the twenty-four categories, choir ranked number 17 in net BOE
  cost.
- Of the twenty-four categories orchestra, ranked number 23 in net BOE
  cost.

Table 8.16   **Net Board of Education Costs in Descending Order**

Rank	Area	Budget Code	Net Board of Education Cost	Participants
1	Football	1,660	88,174	579
2	Boys Basketball	1,655	76,530	501
3	Girls Basketball	1,625	53,913	432
4	Boys Baseball	1,654	42,379	153
5	Band	1,611	39,484	1,255
6	Volleyball	1,641	39,029	487
7	Wrestling	1,672	37,555	232
8	Boys Track	1,669	37,511	252
9	Girls Track	1,639	31,927	289
10	Drama	1,614	31,184	396
11	Softball	1,637	22,867	79
12	Girls Soccer	1,636	19,402	127
13	Boys Soccer	1,666	18,408	130
14	Girls Swimming	1,644	18,057	98
15	Boys Swimming	1,674	17,578	61
16	Speech	1,615	17,388	139
17	Choir	1,612	16,276	581
18	Golf	1,662	14,006	85
19	Cheerleading	1,627	13,107	66
20	Cross Country	1,681	12,204	69
21	Boys Tennis	1,668	11,304	66
22	Girls Tennis	1,638	11,225	62
23	Orchestra	1,613	8,041	195
24	Gymnastics	1,633	7,848	17

Tables 8.17 and 8.18 were developed to demonstrate the number of students participating in each program and the resultant cost per pupil data.

Presenting the same document ranking the various programs according to the number of participants provided interesting additional data.

- Of the twenty-four categories, band ranked number 1 in student participation.
- Of the twenty-four categories, choir ranked number 2 in student participation.
- Of the twenty-four categories, orchestra ranked number 11 in student participation.
- Of the twenty-four categories, the music categories were the only ones that met the entire year.

Table 8.17   Number of Participants in Descending Order

Rank	Area	Budget Code	Net Board of Education Cost	Participants
1	Band	1,611	39,484	1,255
2	Choir	1,612	16,276	581
3	Football	1,660	88,174	579
4	Boys Basketball	1,655	76,530	501
5	Volleyball	1,641	39,029	487
6	Girls Basketball	1,625	53,913	432
7	Drama	1,614	31,184	396
8	Girls Track	1,639	31,927	289
9	Boys Track	1,669	37,511	252
10	Wrestling	1,672	37,555	232
11	Orchestra	1,613	8,041	195
12	Boys Baseball	1,654	42,379	153
13	Speech	1,615	17,388	139
14	Boys Soccer	1,666	18,408	130
15	Girls Soccer	1,636	19,402	127
16	Girls Swimming	1,644	18,057	98
17	Golf	1,662	14,006	85
18	Softball	1,637	22,867	79
19	Cross Country	1,681	12,204	69
20	Cheerleading	1,627	13,107	66
21	Boys Tennis	1,668	11,304	66
22	Girls Tennis	1,638	11,225	62
23	Boys Swimming	1,674	17,578	61
24	Gymnastics	1,633	7,848	17

While table 8.17 provided a significant demonstration of the relative importance of the music program to the students, the addition of a "Cost per Pupil" column in table 8.18 was a major illustration of its financial viability.

Observations on the low cost factor of the music program are demonstrated as follows.

- Of the twenty-four categories, choir ranked number 1 in lowest cost per student.
- Of the twenty-four categories, band ranked number 2 in lowest cost per student.
- Of the twenty-four categories, orchestra ranked number 3 in lowest cost per student.

Table 8.18   Average Participant Cost in Descending Order

Rank	Area	Budget Code	Net Board of Education Cost	Participants	Cost Per Pupil
1	Choir	1,612	16,276	581	$28
2	Band	1,611	39,484	1,255	$31
3	Orchestra	1,613	8,041	195	$41
4	Drama	1,614	31,184	396	$79
5	Volleyball	1,641	39,029	487	$80
6	Girls Track	1,639	31,927	289	$110
7	Girls Basketball	1,625	53,913	432	$125
8	Speech	1,615	17,388	139	$125
9	Boys Soccer	1,666	18,408	130	$142
10	Boys Track	1,669	37,511	252	$149
11	Football	1,660	88,174	579	$152
12	Boys Basketball	1,655	76,530	501	$153
13	Girls Soccer	1,636	19,402	127	$153
14	Wrestling	1,672	37,555	232	$162
15	Golf	1,662	14,006	85	$165
16	Boys Tennis	1,668	11,304	66	$171
17	Cross Country	1,681	12,204	69	$177
18	Girls Tennis	1,638	11,225	62	$181
19	Girls Swimming	1,644	18,057	98	$184
20	Cheerleading	1,627	13,107	66	$199
21	Boys Baseball	1,654	42,379	153	$277
22	Boys Swimming	1,674	17,578	61	$288
23	Softball	1,637	22,867	79	$289
24	Gymnastics	1,633	7,848	17	$462
	Totals		685,397	6,351	$3,923
	Average BOE Cost Per Pupil				$108

In this district the above information and a demonstration of the FTE value of the music teachers was sufficient to have the proposal for participation fees for music removed and the related teaching positions restored. The second case study substantiates the data and demonstrates another motivation for adding music participation fees.

Case Study: Midwest High School

In its *Budget Reduction Summary*, the district recommended the "elimination of cocurricular activities and summer practice aspect of the music program." While it was difficult to predict any positive results of the recommendation of the administration, of even greater significance was the apparent inequity of adding a student participation fee to continue the summer program. This could be demonstrated by examining the comparative per pupil costs from the document entitled "Public Schools District News Notice," in which the district delineated extracurricular per pupil expense as indicated in table 8.19.

Observations:

- There were 868 students participating in eighteen seasonal activities under the leadership of sixty-three staff.
- The ratio of student participants to staff was 13.8:1.
- The total cost of these activities was $98,180, excluding staff salaries.
- Per pupil costs for the eighteen activities varied from a high of $833.94 for hockey to a low of $39.46 for boys' golf.
- The average per pupil cost for all activities was $113.11, excluding salaries.
- A more accurate figure of per pupil costs was reflected in the total budgetary figure for the eighteen activities, including salaries as seen opposite.

Table 8.19   Extracurricular Costs per Pupil* (in Descending Order by Pupil Cost)

Activity	Students	Staff	Ratio	Cost*	Cost per Pupil
1. Hockey	33	3	11.0	$27,520	$833.94
2. Boys Swim/Dive	9	1	9.0	2,445	271.67
3. Boys Cross Country	8	1	8.0	1,275	159.38
4. Girls Swim/Dive	28	2	14.0	2,750	98.21
5. Girls Cross Country	14	1	14.0	1,375	98.21
6. Girls Basketball	80	5	16.0	7,525	94.06
7. Softball	32	3	10.7	3,010	94.06
8. Football	153	11	13.9	13,950	91.18
9. Boys Basketball	82	5	16.4	7,455	90.91
10. Baseball	33	3	11.0	2,950	89.39
11. Volleyball	82	6	13.7	7,250	88.41
12. Wrestling	44	4	11.0	3,450	78.41
13. Boys Track/Field	52	4	13.0	3,975	76.44
14. Girls Track/Field	57	4	14.3	4,010	70.35
15. Boys Tennis	40	3	13.3	2,720	68.00
16. Girls Golf	29	2	14.5	1,855	63.97
17. Girls Tennis	46	3	15.3	2,850	61.96
18. Boys Golf	46	2	23.0	1,815	39.46
Totals	868	63		$98,180	
Average			13.8		$113.11

*Costs do not include salaries.

Total Budget	$335,132
Total Revenues	49,170
Net Board of Education Cost	$285,962

- With 868 students participating in the eighteen seasonal activities, the actual average cost per participant was $329.45.

While it must be understood that music is essentially a curricular subject, it is evident that some of its cocurricular and extracurricular events were included in the district budget related to those expenses. This was particularly apparent in the budgetary treatment of the summer music program and allocation of extracurricular stipends provided to music performance staff.

It should be noted that there was no intent to compare music and athletics in their philosophical or curricular content, cast any negative character on either, or suggest which was more important. It was true in fact that students for the most part were interested in and benefited from both. Rather, it was the purpose here to demonstrate the inequity of charging fees for participation in music that was in its primary content curricular. (As a matter of demonstrating our intent not to compete with or negate the validity of the athletic program, I asked parents to stand if they had students in both music and athletics. Nearly every parent stood.)

Specifically, with 897 students participating in cocurricular and/or extracurricular music at a cost of $30,000 for a full year, the average participant cost to the district was $33.44. The average cost of an athletic activity as compared to participation in music was approximately 10:1. Further, the 897 music participants were provided with only 3.5 total FTE (a ratio of 256:1), and were not allowed daily rehearsal (practice) times until grade 10.

It is apparent that any fee charged to student participants in music was really an effort on the part of the administration to balance the expense of the other eighteen activities; specifically, the district was asking the music program to subsidize the athletic program.

The music program was reinstated and participation fees for music dropped.

THE DANGERS OF FUND-RAISING

Historically music booster organizations have been primarily fund-raisers. This is perhaps the primary distinction between a booster organization and a music coalition. In some cases, boosters have been so effective at raising "volunteer taxes" that administrators have proposed not funding music programs simply because the district knew of the boosters' effectiveness at raising money for the program. In an increasing number of cases, boosters are even being asked to fund the teaching position(s).

> The willingness of a district to fund a music curriculum is
> often in direct relationship to the perceived ability of the
> boosters to raise their own support.
>
> * * *
>
> The more money you raise, the less you are apt to
> get from the district budget!

It is my recommendation (as a music educator and former school board member) that fund-raising be restricted to those aspects of the music program that are extracurricular. By funding curricular or cocurricular aspects of the program with fund-raising activities you are demonstrating your tacit approval that music education is extracurricular. This undermines the credibility of the music program as academic or core curriculum.

There have been instances when a music coalition has successfully acted to fund a position for a new aspect of the music program, such starting a new string curriculum. This can be very effective. However, I strongly recommend that you do this only when the administration agrees by official board action to assume the funding of the program within one or two years.

DECLINING ENROLLMENT

One of the difficult problems faced by many school districts is a declining student population. Funding of a school district is based on the number of students attending schools within the district. Fewer students means less money. Less money means budget cuts, and that usually means a reduction in the number of teaching positions.

Under these circumstances the choice to cut music teachers is often a philosophical decision based on the presumed assumption that music programs are the most expensive. As previously noted, this is rarely the case. No cuts in music faculty can be justified unless enrollments in the music program are also declining. In fact, the opposite is often the case. For some unknown reason our experience has been that music enrollments often maintain the strength of their enrollments during times of declining district enrollment, and sometimes actually increase.

It is important that enrollment data is maintained to demonstrate the numerical health of the program and the FTE value of the average music teacher. This is the key to maintaining faculty positions in the presence of declining enrollment trends.

THE STUDY HALL GAME: HIDDEN AGENDAS

About the only educational program that I have found to be more cost-effective than a music program is study hall. As part of a cost-saving effort, the administration in one school district proposed the elimination of four vocal performing groups as part of their recommendation that *all* 1,500 students in the high school be required to take a minimum of one study hall per six-period day. The parent committees' response (impact statements) follows.

Administrative proposal:

- Eliminate four vocal performing groups at the high school.
- All high school students (1,500) will be required to take a minimum of one study hall per six-period day.

Impact statements:

- The student load for an average classroom teacher is 125.
- The current high school choral director (1.0 FTE) has a student load of 600. A student load of 600 equates to 4.8 FTE classroom teachers. The reverse economic effect is obvious, except for the minimum requirement of one study hall per day per student.
- The elimination of 352 students from participation in the choral program (four groups) provides no savings to the district since the 248 students left in the program still equate to an overload.
- There will also be cuts in the instrumental music program.
- The only cost savings factor comes with the study halls which will be staffed with 1.0 FTE and contain 250 students each period.
- The composition of students per hour in study hall is demonstrated in table 8.20.
- Since it is obvious that the administration does not philosophically support the validity of study hall as an appropriate academic function, it would appear that there are in fact only two real purposes to requiring study hall of all students.

  o To require an additional forty-five nonmusic students per hour to attend study hall, equating to a total savings of 2.1 FTE for the district.

Table 8.20   Study Hall Students

Normal Study Hall Students	100
New Nonmusic Students	45
Former Vocal Music Students	59
Former Instrumental Music Students	46
Total Study Hall Students (Proposed)	250

o To eliminate the opportunity for 630 students (6 hours x 105 instrumental and choral students) to participate in the music program of the high school.

The elimination of the teaching positions specified would have equated to a 50 percent cut in music staffing. A major question remained for the parents: why was it that such a high percentage of music positions were targeted for elimination when the financial "crisis" suggested by the district was so small? Upon further investigation it was discovered that there was a tenured teacher that the administration had wanted to fire for a long time. The financial "crisis" provided the perfect opportunity. However, the district would have needed to cut 50 percent of the teaching staff to get to that individual. The astounding thing was that there seemed to be little or no concern for the result on the students. The parents made sure that the decision was not carried out, and the program was saved.

Tenure does not protect an incompetent teacher.
It exposes an inadequate system of evaluation of the program and the faculty.

9

Implementing the Process

Whether you are attempting to establish a new program, prevent cuts to a current one, or requesting additional funds to meet the needs of a growing program, the process is much the same. Generally, there are four stages through which you will go.

Stage 1: The collection and interpretation of data
Stage 2: The preparation of the proposal
Stage 3: The presentation of the proposal
Stage 4: Follow-up

STAGE 1: THE COLLECTION AND INTERPRETATION OF DATA

If your music coalition is functioning as it should you will have at least one member of the music coalition representing the music program at each meeting of the school board. In so doing you should be aware of the current philosophical direction and financial status of the district. You should provide regular reports to coalition members through the music coalition newsletter. These reports should include information related to any proposals under consideration by the administration and board, a summary of assumptions related to adoption of the district budget, and any surveys under consideration by the district. To be most effective as a music advocate you must be familiar with the following information.

- "Educese"—the vocabulary of educators used in nearly every policy and budget discussion (see glossary)

- The chronology of events that occurs in the development of the district budget
- The (voting) position of each member of the board on each proposal under consideration

If you are making funding requests it is best to submit them either in the spring, before the budget discussions begin, or immediately at the beginning of the fiscal year. Here are six rules that I find helpful in increasing financial allocations for the music program.

Rule 1: Always ask for more than you expect to get! I maintain a five-year budget development plan that includes program maintenance and growth (staffing), capital expense (equipment and supplies), and other aspects of the program (miscellaneous expenses, travel, etc.). To be completely honest, this also gives my administration something to cut and takes them out of the political dilemma of "always giving the music program everything they want."

Rule 2: Run out of money before the end of the year. This demonstrates that you needed more than you were given; that is, the administration cut too many items from your previous budget request. Your administration most likely has certain discretionary funds or powers to provide funds for end-of-the-year emergencies. Programs that do not spend all of their budget funds by the end of the year usually lose those monies and have their budgets reduced for the next fiscal year.

Rule 3: Spend your money evenly over the year. Every year there are those who come to the realization that they have a large portion of their budget that has not been spent. Then they make this sudden attempt to spend quickly. To the administration this is an indication of poor planning on the part of the music (or other) department and leads to the assumption that you do not need as much funding in future years. On the other hand, if you do not spend your money it will be given to another department or put back into the general fund.

Rule 4: Be able to justify each expenditure. This can and should be also be clarified in a summary annual report.

Rule 5: Have a long-term capital plan. A five-year plan is minimal. For purchases like music instruments, a ten-year plan is more feasible. If you have an instrument preventive maintenance schedule you can extend the life of instruments indefinitely. You should also demonstrate this in the purchase of music, uniforms/robes, and so on.

Rule 6: Draw pictures with your budget requests. What you are doing here is making impact statements. You should demonstrate the impact on the students if the request is denied. See table 9.1, in which the request is for $1,800 for the purchase of music for one choir for one year.

If you are dealing with an issue of crisis management, you will need to define the specific issues: educational reform, budget cuts, hidden agendas,

Table 9.1   Budget Request: Choral Music

First Period Choir	
50 students	50
4 concerts	x 4
New songs per concert (in addition to current library)	x 6
Cost per copy	$1.50
Total Costs	$1,800
Possible impact(s) on students if denied:	
Fewer students will be admitted to first period choir	
Students may perform fewer concerts	
Students will not have individual copies	

and so on. You will then use the appropriate information to analyze the situation and develop impact statements related to the specific issues being addressed.

Basic to all of this will be the collection of data on the public school music participation survey (appendix A). In addition you will need the following information:

- Copies of proposals and documents related to the specific issues;
- Assumptions related to the proposals before the board;
- Results of any surveys or other documentation related to the proposals, including district mission statements, philosophies, and goals.

STAGE 2: THE PREPARATION OF THE PROPOSAL

Using the information collected (see appendix A), analyze the data in order to demonstrate the following factors related to the music program.

- The number of students participating in each area of the music program (general music, band, choir, orchestra)
- The number of students participating in each grade in each aspect of the music program
- The percentage of eligible students participating in the program at each grade level, each school level (elementary, middle or junior high, senior), and in the total district
- The attrition rates between grades and school levels (if the enrollment figures are maintained from year to year)
- The actual number of FTE assigned to each area of the music curriculum
- The FTE value of the average music performance teacher compared to the classroom teacher

- The financial loss that will be incurred if large music classes are lost because of the (full or partial) elimination of the (elementary) feeder system
- The impact (loss of students) if any specific area of the curriculum is unavailable, and the effect that will have on class size increases in non-music courses

Once you have collected and analyzed the data you begin developing your impact statements and begin to write your proposal. A typical proposal contains the following information.

- Title: A Status Report on Music in the ABC District Schools
- Introduction: In this section you should include a summary of recent research on the importance of music education for all children. Make sure that you distinguish between collaborative and causal statements. (See discussion on using research effectively in chapter 4.)
- History of Music in the District: Here you should include a listing of significant events or recognition that provides the district with recognition of its music program, particularly regional, national, or international recognition and awards. This could include teachers, but should emphasize student achievement.
- The second thing to include here is a listing of any previous cuts made to the music program, so that you can demonstrate the cumulative effect of any currently proposed actions that may negatively impact the program.
- Administrative Proposal: In this section summarize the administrative proposal, listing each item that does or may include music. Include a financial total of any cuts and a listing of possible hidden cuts.
- Assumptions: List the budgetary or other assumptions made or implied in the administrative proposal. I usually include the following assumptions if they are not in the administrative document.

  o The primary emphasis in determining what reductions to make should be placed on maintaining the quality of instruction in the classroom.
  o Programs with fewer pupils impacted adversely should be reduced or eliminated before programs with lower cost-benefit ratios.
  o Long-term financial savings are not guaranteed by program reductions, but may be realized by investing in those programs that have the potential for the greatest student-faculty ratios.

- Short- and Long-Term Impacts:

  o Faculty: In this section include relevant information related to the number of actual FTE allocated to each music area at each of the educational levels, student-faculty ratios in music, whether teachers are teaching in areas outside of their specialized training, and other issues that surface during your data collection.

- o Curriculum: The primary issue here is normally the failure to recognize the differences in music as curricular, cocurricular, and extracurricular. Also included are such issues as the absence of a written curriculum, a system of assessment of student achievement in music, the absence or inadequacy of a general music curriculum, and the failure to begin the instrumental and choral music performance programs no later than grade 5.
- o Student Participation: Use the results of the public school music participation survey to provide graphic information related to the number of students participating in each area of the music curriculum. This should include the distinctive characteristics of enrollment by school and grade, percentages of participation, rates of attrition, and the potential for growth. (See "Reverse Economics" in chapter 8.)
- o Economy: Using data from the survey, indicate the FTE value of the music performance teachers as compared to classroom teachers, detailing the impact that the loss of students in music classes will have on class size and the need to hire nonmusic classroom teachers.

- Summary, Conclusions, and Recommendations:

  - o Identified Issues: During your study you will discover several issues that prevent or inhibit the ability of students to participate in music. List these individually.
  - o Task Force: You want to request the formation of an official task force so that your coalition can be involved in the entire process of solving the identified issues. Membership on the task force should include balanced representation from the central and site administration (all levels), music teachers, classroom teachers, and the community (all schools and levels).

STAGE 3: THE PRESENTATION OF THE PROPOSAL

Once your proposal(s) have been developed it is important that you recognize several issues that may affect the outcome. Among those are the following.

The Role of the Various Constituents

- Music Coalition: One of the primary reasons that you form a coalition is to broaden your base of political power. The more you can facilitate their involvement the more likely you are to have long-term success.

- School Board: These are your neighbors. They want to do what is right, but they can only act on the information provided. Therefore, it is important that you have good information. Oftentimes the most important information is just enough people present at the meeting to provide enough political pressure to indicate the importance of your program to the community, that is, to get enough votes to win. Remember the vote does not have to be unanimous, but only a majority.
- Administration: There are basically two types of administrators: authoritarian and collaborative. Be open with both types, but recognize that the more authoritarian the operational style of the administrator is the more important the visible "vote" of the people will be. Collaborative administrators may even request that you make your public presentation so that they have a means of demonstrating their desire to serve the community.
- Music Teachers: It is my observation and preference that music teachers are excluded from active participation in the *public* advocacy process. In the first place, anything they say or do is normally interpreted as either self-serving (conflict of interest) or insubordinate. I have seen too many cases where teachers could not control their tongues in a public meeting and have ended up destroying the process to the demise of the program.
- Consultant: In some cases you may seek the advice of an outside consultant. If you are in a proactive setting it may be desirable to have the consultant meet with the board or administration. That usually works best if the administration or board recommends it or has previously endorsed the process. In a reactive situation (action against an administrative proposal), it is normally best that the consultant not present directly to the board. However, a general presentation open to the public is not only normal, but also proper. This includes an invitation for the media to attend. If you consider hiring a consultant, the invitation should come from the music coalition, not the music educator. This is for the protection of the teacher and the empowerment of the coalition. The itinerary or agenda I use is included in appendix B.

System Protocol within the District

As you advocate for your music program, it is advisable to follow several specific practices:

- Have at least one member of the music coalition at each meeting of the school board.
- Be open with your activities. If you intend to take a position against a proposal, be open about your intent and process.

- Meet with board first. They are your legal representatives.
- Provide all information to the administration. If possible, meet with them in an attempt to address your issues privately. The intent here is to avoid a public confrontation that may place them in such a defensive position that they may lose face if they cave in to a "special interest group."
- If you are unsuccessful in convincing the board and administration in a private manner, you may need to go public. It is best to get on the official meeting agenda. In some cases they may limit you to speaking in a public forum. This may limit your time, so be prepared to have your presentation divided between several consecutive speakers.
- Provide the board and administration with all printed documents or your formal proposal well before the meeting so that they are not able to delay a decision because they have not had time to review your information.
- *Depending on the seriousness of the crisis or chronology of the decision-making process, have as many members of the music coalition and community as possible attend the meeting in support of your presentation.*

STAGE 4: FOLLOW-UP

Once you have completed your proposal and presented it to the administration and board, the decision has hopefully gone the direction you intended. This is not just a time to celebrate your victory. It is a time to be aware of other actions that are still to be made.

If your negotiations at this point have been primarily at the level of the board and administration, you need to remain aware of those decisions that may still be made at the local site level (see "Central and Site-Based Management" in chapter 3). Be particularly alert of this if district budget deliberations include changing class sizes or increases in the staffing ratio.

In other instances you may have certain administrators who feel they have been publicly embarrassed or angry. This could lead to a revenge cycle in which they return year after year recommending cuts in your program. Certain administrators may implement changes at the local site level that can negatively impact your program. In one situation, for example, the orchestra was "inadvertently" left off the registration schedule at the local high school. Students soon discovered this, but it was "too late" to reprint the registration packet. Several students ended up with class schedules in which courses they were required to take for graduation were at the same hour as orchestra. Other examples that have occurred include the following:

- Scheduling of other courses in the music room(s)
- Adding activity or "pay-to-play" fees for participation in music
- Making site-based decisions without providing due notice to the teachers or public

After this process is completed, it would be wise to have some type of official expression of thanks extended to the board and administration. Public affirmations, letters to editors, a "thank you" time of refreshments at the end of a subsequent board meeting, and other means as determined by the music coalition to be appropriate would be beneficial to reestablishing positive relationships.

> Maintaining professional relationships is a lot easier if
> you avoid personal attacks and name-calling.
> In other words: *Be professional!*

DEVELOPING AN ANNUAL REPORT

Why? Marketing! Developing an annual report is simply the best way to keep your administration and school board informed about the importance and status of your music program. It can help establish its validity as a core value in the community.

Assessment! It will give you a more accurate picture of what you program really is accomplishing. It will provide you with the information you need to move your program forward.

Your report should contain information on various components of the program, achievements, and any issues related to the current status of the program and its potential for growth. Some suggestions are categorized below.

Faculty

- List significant recognition of individual faculty, such as awards, honors, publications, and years-of-service milestones.
- Identify the number of FTE in each area of the curriculum.
- Summarize the student-faculty ratios in each area of the curriculum.

Curriculum

- List significant accomplishments of performance groups: festivals, contests, and tours.

- List significant accomplishments of individual student performers: solo and ensemble contests, and scholarships to graduating seniors.
- Summarize general academic success of music students: honor roll, average GPA, and SAT/ACT scores.
- Summarize student completion of music curriculum competencies.
- Summarize the performance events of the year: cocurricular and extracurricular.

Student Participation

- Summarize student enrollments in music classes: general music, band, choir, and orchestra.
- Summarize the average class sizes in each area of the music curriculum.
- Identify percentages of student participation by grade and school.
- Identify attrition rates that exceed 15 percent between any two grades as areas of concern.
- Summarize results of exit interviews of students who drop music performance classes.
- Summarize the average class sizes in each area of the curriculum.

Economics

- Determine the FTE value of the average music performance teacher.
- Summarize the expenditure of budgetary funds.
- Demonstrate need for budgetary funds in the coming year.

Music Coalition

- The administrative liaison committee of the music coalition should prepare the report in cooperation with the music teachers.
- The administrative liaison committee should present an abbreviated oral report at a public meeting of the school board, based on the formal written report.
- The report should summarize the activities of the music coalition and its contributions to the district, including fund-raising.

Finally—don't forget to express your appreciation to the administration, board, and community for accepting the report and past support for the program!

10

Music Advocacy: Moving from Survival to Vision

Over the last several decades music advocacy has assumed a variety of approaches. It is my observation that these have essentially fallen into two categories: reactive and proactive.

THE REACTIVE APPROACH

This is the most common approach to music advocacy. It is identifiable by one or more of the following characteristics.

- It assumes a reactionary posture of maintaining the status quo, often accompanied by a sense of denial in which it is assumed that the program is safe from attack.
- There is usually not a functioning written curriculum. If there is, it rarely is being applied systematically across the district and almost never has an adequate process of assessment in place to demonstrate curricular viability.
- There is little or no consistent curricular scope and sequence between grades and feeder schools.
- There is no distinction between those aspects of the music program that are curricular, cocurricular, or extracurricular.
- The program tends to be teacher- or director-centered, often with the same content repeated year after year with little or no assessment or improvement.
- Teachers tend to operate autonomously with little accountability for student achievement other than bringing a trophy or superior rating back from the most recent event.

- No records are kept as to the level of student participation or attrition.
- If a community coalition is present, it is normally limited to fund-raising activities, and rarely composed of a unified constituency representing all aspects of the music program.
- Its relationship to the district is often adversarial.

I compare the reactive approach to a person sitting in the middle of a lake in a boat with only one oar: the program just keeps going, but doesn't necessarily make any significant progress in curricular improvement or levels of student participation.

THE PROACTIVE APPROACH

On the other hand, as the advocacy movement picks up the second oar, it has begun to mature and has become much more effective. It is making progress as a proactive force, even upstream, and is identifiable by one or more of the following characteristics.

- It is organized and unified in its efforts.
- It is connected with other local, regional, and national coalitions.
- It is becoming more prepared and strategic in its efforts.
- It is more informed about the value of music education for its children, from both philosophical and practical perspectives.
- Teachers are viewing themselves as music educators, not just general music, band, choir, or orchestra teachers.
- Music teachers are becoming less competitive with each other and more focused on student-centered decision making and competence achievement.
- It is establishing positive, collaborative working relationships with educators and legislators and has extensive involvement with the local school district.

The key to becoming a proactive influence for music education is the development of a "dream list." It is more often referred to as a long-term plan. Do you know what you want your program to look like in the next five years? Ten years? Start now! Here are a few hints to get you started. (Note: A significant part of your initial plan will be developing a profile of the current status of the music program and any factors that may inhibit progress.)

- Establish a unified, district-wide music coalition.
- Determine the FTE value of your music teachers.
- Create a profile of current enrollments in band, choir, and orchestra.

- Determine the student-to-faculty ratio (SFR) of music teachers to eligible students.
- Develop a written curriculum, with adequate assessment procedures.
- Define the various aspects of your music program as to its curricular, cocurricular, and extracurricular components.
- Analyze the current status of the music budget (average allocation per student in each category of the budget).

Once you have established a profile of the current status of your program, begin to develop a dream list of ideas for improving and expanding music opportunities for students. You are asking only one question: *If there were no limitations of any kind, what do you envision to be the ideal music program for your district?* Here are a few more hints to take you through that process.

- There is only one rule in this process: there should be no limitations on ideas (ideological, philosophical, staffing, financial, etc.).
- Facilitate brainstorming sessions with music teachers (by area), the music coalition, and the administration.
- Facilitate similar sessions with members of the administration and non-music teachers to determine their dreams, but also to learn what the issues may be that could prevent you from achieving your dreams.
- Prioritize the list and develop your long-term plan.

Appendix A:
The Public School Music Participation Survey

The Public School Music Participation Survey is a result of over twenty-five years of working with community groups and school music programs. It has been effective in the analysis of a single school or district. It may also be used in the development of statewide data: the Georgia Project, which focused on the arts in general, not just music, compiled information from thirty-three districts serving over 641,000 students.

The survey shown in figure A.1 will help you demonstrate that music is beneficial not only to the student but also to the entire district and community! Will completing this survey help save or create music programs?

Yes! The information requested in part 1 (pages 1–2) is designed help you understand the school district as a whole and analyze issues that arise in the development or defense of a music program.

The information collected in part 2 (page 3) relates specifically to the music program and is to be completed by *each* music teacher. If music teachers complete part 2 at the beginning and the end of each school year, you'll have a statistical profile of student participation and attrition, faculty loads, and the economic viability of the music program. And, even more importantly, you'll have the data you need to examine student attrition and its causes and to defend your school or district's music program in times of financial threat.

All information requested in part 1 is available through the central administration of your school district. By law, it is public information, so your request for these materials may not be legally denied.

I recommend your music coalition establish a policy with your school board and administration to regularly collect this data for an annual report on the status of the music program. If collection becomes district policy, this data can be included as part of its required reporting procedures. Even if no such policy is adopted, a member of the music coalition statistics and finance committee in each school or curricular area should be responsible for collecting the completed forms from the central administration and all music teachers.

(Note: Some additional information is mentioned in the general survey instructions: list of schools, list of music teachers [with FTE assignments], school board documents related to music, etc. These materials should be maintained by the music coalition for reference because they may assist you in interpreting the data or defending your program in a case of crisis.)

GENERAL SURVEY INSTRUCTIONS

1. Please complete all information as requested and check for accuracy before returning surveys.
2. Please *print* or *type* all information.
3. Please provide copies of all budget and/or budget cut information and related publicity.
4. Please provide a separate list of all music teachers in the (school or) district.
5. Provide a list of all schools that are a part of the district.

Instructions for Part 1

Pages 1–2 are to be completed by one individual. Information in this section, which relates to the school district as a whole, will be available from the central administration office.

Page 1

1. Enter the academic year, district name, and district number, and the name and daytime phone number of the person completing the survey.
2. Enter the number of students enrolled in each grade. Do *not* include those students enrolled in special education, unless "mainstreamed." If possible, attach a copy of the district enrollment census summary.
3. Indicate the starting grade for middle (junior high) school and high school.
4. Indicate the appropriate (yes/no) response to the next four questions. The starting grade for band and orchestra as regular classes is the first grade in which students are not pulled out of another class. Generally this is the first year of middle or junior high school.
5. Enter the average overall class size. This is the number of students in the average classroom, not the entire grade. Also provide this by curricular area if available.

Page 2

1. Teacher information: Enter the district number.

   a. The questions related to minutes/teaching periods are the basis for how your district defines one full-time classroom teacher, or 1.0 full-time equivalent (FTE) teacher. Include any responsibility given to the teacher that is part of the (1.0 FTE teacher point) teaching load.

In some cases this may include study hall, supervisory duties, or other nonmusic classes.

b. Do *not* include extra-duty assignments that are not a part of the regular (salaried) teacher load, planning time, or nonteaching assignments.

c. Indicate the average teacher salary. Do *not* include benefits or extra-duty stipends.

2. Socioeconomic information: Please provide the median family income in the district and the race/ethnic proportions as a percentage of student population.

Instructions for Part 2

Page 3

Make copies of this page to be completed by every full-time or part-time music teacher (general music, band, choir, orchestra, etc.) and each music supervisor/coordinator or music department/area chair. This section requests information related to students and teachers in music. To ensure accuracy, enter the district name and district number before you duplicate and distribute this page.

1. Enter the name and employment status (full or part time) of each teacher. If part time, enter the percent of the part-time assignment.

2. Teacher load information: Enter the school name. Make a separate line entry for *each* class (course subject) and/or load-bearing assignment or responsibility. Do *not* enter the school code number.

   a. Enter the length of the class or responsibility in minutes.
   b. Enter the number of times per week that the class or responsibility meets.

3. Student participation information:

   a. For *each* class indicated under the teacher load, enter the number of students from *each* grade that participates in each class.
   b. Enter the total number of students for each class or responsibility listed.
   c. Please do not combine similar courses into one calculation; for example, do *not* combine students from different performing ensembles on a single line unless the student is in both ensembles.

Please do *not* guess or estimate! As with any statistical study, the usefulness of the information collected depends upon accuracy. Please work with *each* of the people involved in your survey to ensure they provide the most complete and accurate data possible. The future of your school district's music programming depends upon it!

Return *all* completed survey forms to:

Name:	Telephone:
Address:	Email:
City/State/Zip:	Fax:

Public School Music Participation Survey – Part I: School District Information (Page 1)

(PLEASE PRINT OR TYPE ALL INFORMATION)   For Academic Year _____ - _____

District Name:		District Number:		Person Completing Survey:	
				Daytime Telephone: ( ) -	

District Enrollment Census (excluding Special Education)

Grade:	K	1	2	3	4	5	6	7	8	9	10	11	12	Total
Enrollment:														

What is the starting grade for Middle/Junior High School?

What is the starting grade for High School?

Are elementary general music classes used as a means to provide planning time for classroom teachers?   Yes   No

Is there an elementary band or orchestra curriculum?

If yes, is it used as a means to provide planning time for classroom teachers?

What is the first grade in which band, orchestra and/or choir are regular (non-pull out) classes?

Class Size Information

	Elementary School	Middle/Junior High	Senior High
Average Class Size (by level)			

Figure A.1a.   Public School Music Participation Survey

Public School Music Participation Survey – Part I: School District Information (Page 2)

(PLEASE PRINT OR TYPE ALL INFORMATION)   For Academic Year _____ - _____

Teacher Information: (Please provide the information requested as it relates to a *full time equivalent teacher position (1.0 FTE)*

	Elementary School	Middle/Junior High School	High School

District Number: [   ]

What is the number of teaching minutes (student contact time) per week?
(Please do *not* include planning time?)
[ ] [ ] [ ]

What is the number of teaching periods (student contact time) per week?
(Please do *not* include planning time)
[ ] [ ] [ ]

What is the average full time teacher salary (1.0 FTE, without benefits or extra-duty stipends)? $ [   ]

Socio-Economic Information:

What are the racial/ethnic proportions (%) in the district?

African American [ ]
American Indian [ ]
Asian [ ]
Hispanic [ ]
White/Anglo [ ]
Other [ ]

What is the average family income in the district?

$ [   ]

Figure A.1b.   Public School Music Participation Survey

Public School Music Participation Survey – Part II: School District Information (Page 3)

(PLEASE PRINT OR TYPE ALL INFORMATION)

For Academic Year _____ – _____

Music Teacher, Enrollment and Curriculum Information

District Number: ☐

Teacher Last Name: _____   First Name: _____

Indicate Employment Status:

Full Time ☐   Part Time ☐   If part time, indicate % of full time: _____

Teacher Load Information				Office Use		Student Participation													
						Students Enrolled *by Grade* for *Each* Class													
School Name	Course/ Subject	Length (Min)	Times per Week	School Code	Load %	K	1	2	3	4	5	6	7	8	9	10	11	12	Total

Figure A.1c.   Public School Music Participation Survey

Appendix B:
Consultant Process:
Itinerary and Agenda

*Consultant responsibility

Before arrival:

___Set up meeting dates, locations, and times.
___Arrange for equipment needs for each meeting:
  ___Large projection screen
  ___Six-foot or eight-foot table
  ___Lapel microphone for large group meeting(s)

___Have information survey forms completed as appropriate (returned by _____).
___Collect and forward articles, school board work documents, budget proposals, cut proposals, educational reform, and any other materials related to the current situation.
___Send a list of all music teachers in the district.
___Send a list of all schools in the district.
___Meet with music dealers, asking for voluntary contributions.
___*Formulate a rough draft of status report.

Day 1:

___Arrive in _____
4:00–6:30 p.m.: Meeting with music teachers (3 hours)
  ___*Present the schedule for the consultation
  ___*Review the situation and purpose for consultation
  ___*Uniting teachers/Empowering parents
  ___*Brainstorming on district—history of music, honors and awards, confirm statistics, develop "dream list," define issues

Day 2:

   ___*(Finish) Analyze data and configure the status report (cost-benefit analysis)*

Day 3:

9:30–11:30 a.m.: Open meeting with community (parents, teachers, public)

   ___*Discuss why they are there and give them the schedule.*
   ___*Go through (empowering) PowerPoint as appropriate.*
   ___*Clarify specified and hidden issues.*
   ___*Ask for questions. (Observe for selecting leadership team candidates.)*
   ___Have someone "pass the hat" during the question time.
   ___Have people write down their names, addresses, and telephone numbers if they wish to be involved in the process.
   ___Have people sign on a separate list if they wish to serve on the leadership team.
   ___*See about organizing music boosters (and/or into committees).*

11:30 a.m.–2:30 p.m.: Meeting with leadership team (2–4 hours)

   ___Order in refreshments/lunch.
   ___Proofread the report, edit, and reprint.
   ___Set up strategies according to local needs.
   ___Assign specific tasks to specific people as team determines needs.

      ___Telephone banks
      ___Administrative meetings
      ___Music coalition organizing

   ___Select key speaker(s) for presenting the proposal to the board and/or administration.
   ___Request task force?

Day 4:

   ___Return to home office.

Follow-up:

   ___*Continued availability for assistance as necessary*
   ___*Advice, interpretation of issues, further consultation, speech writing*

Appendix C:
The Georgia Project:
A Status Report on Arts Education in the State of Georgia

EXECUTIVE SUMMARY

The Georgia Project: A Status Report on Arts Education in the State of Georgia is a 155-page statistical profile of arts education in Georgia public schools (GPS). Data for the report were gathered from:

- 33 study districts (seventeen over 10,000 student population; sixteen under 10,000)
- 841 schools (K–12)
- 1,705 arts teachers
- 641,635 students (51 percent of total GPS student population)

The report details student participation rates, course offerings and curriculum, and staffing and funding of arts programs. In an addendum to the report, selected data from the *Georgia Public Education Report Card* (GPERC) are compared with data gathered for the status report. Statistically significant relationships were found between arts program profiles in the status report and demographic/academic data in the GPERC.

RESULTS

Analysis of the arts programs in the thirty-three study districts reveals the following:

Arts Staffing

- Arts staffing ratios vary tremendously from district to district, with no apparent consistency among large or small districts, suggesting a lack of any uniform and/or adequate standard for staffing of the arts curriculum.
- Nearly $2 million is spent annually for 47.09 FTE of arts teacher time allocated to non-arts duties, including travel time, instruction of non-arts subjects, hallway supervision, and so forth.

Arts Curriculum

- As with arts staffing, variability in the offering and scheduling of arts curricula among and within districts suggests a lack of standards for the arts.

In general, there appear to be significant issues of inequity for student opportunities to participate in arts programs within the study districts. Inequities pertain to the variety and extent of arts courses available, and may be correlated with district size and other factors such as socioeconomic and ethnic characteristics of each district.

Student Participation

- Student participation in the arts is generally low and varies widely from district to district.
- Two-thirds or more of eligible students do *not* participate in elective arts in any way.
- Attrition rates in music performance (band, choir, orchestra) classes are generally high, especially between grades 8 and 9 (middle school to high school), where they averaged 43 percent.

Economics

- Average student load for music performance teachers in the thirty-three study districts is 171 students, compared to an average student load of 144 for all teachers. Actual student loads vary drastically from district to district.
- The excess student load for music performance teachers equates to a 1.2 FTE value to the district; that is, they carry the student load of 1.2 FTE for each 1.0 FTE paid.
- The 1.2 FTE financial value of music performance teachers helps to maintain smaller class sizes in other academic areas and saves over $3.6 million annually.

- Increasing student participation in music performance would multiply this economic savings; just reducing student attrition in band to a level more in line with national standards of excellence (15 percent maximum per year) would result in 68,496 additional band students and potential savings of over $4 million annually.

CORRELATION WITH GEORGIA
PUBLIC EDUCATION REPORT CARD

The addendum used regression analysis to examine relationships between data from the status report and the GPERC. The analysis found statistically significant relationships as indicated in table C.1.

While the above findings do not prove a cause-and-effect relationship, they do indicate that "strong arts programs need not come at the expense of academic achievement. Rather, the arts are an important factor in achieving academic excellence."

Further studies are recommended to clarify issues raised in the status report and the addendum, especially regarding issues of equal access by students to opportunities in the arts.

Table C.1   Relationship Descriptor

	p-value	Confidence
Districts that make staffing and funding of their arts programs a priority tend to have higher overall rates of student participation in the arts and higher rates of arts student retention (lower rates of attrition).	.08	92%
Such districts tend to have lower dropout rates in grades 9–12 and thus keep their students in school longer and graduate more of them.	.08	92%
Their students tend to score higher on achievement and performance tests, such as the SAT and the Georgia High School Graduation Test.	.03–.08	92–97%
They tend to graduate more of their students with college prep diplomas, percentages increasing with diversity of arts curricula and percent of students participating.	.007	99+%
The above relationships may not apply equally across socioeconomic and ethnic groups. Specifically, the study found that arts student retention rates are negatively correlated with both ethnic minority percentage of enrollment and percentage of enrollment eligible for subsidized lunch (a measure of district affluence).	.003–.01	99+%

Glossary

Note: Assessment terms in italics and their definitions come from Edward Asmus's article, "Music Assessment Concepts," in the September 1999 issue of *Music Educators Journal*.

After School Programs: This reform movement supports the concept of educational funding for programs that are outside the regular school day. The intent, in part, is positive—to keep children off the streets—but music is often one of the curricular areas suggested for placement outside the regular curricular day, and that can mean death to the program. (See **cocurricular** and **extracurricular**.)

Alternative Assessment: Any assessment technique other than traditional paper-and-pencil tests that uses strategies for collecting and analyzing information.

Alternative Scheduling: This reform movement term includes a variety of class scheduling alternatives, including block scheduling, trimesters, and "skinny" class periods. Alternative scheduling may greatly increase potential scheduling conflicts for music courses, and daily contact time for music students may be reduced or changed to alternate days.

Appropriated Fund Balance: The portion of the fund balance assigned and restricted to a particular purpose or use.

Assessment: The collection, analysis, interpretation, and application of information about student performance or program effectiveness in order to make educational decisions.

Authentic Assessment: Assessment techniques that gather information about students' ability to perform tasks that are found in real-world situations.

Average: Using financial averages to create school budgets is an act of economic convenience—and could be interpreted as "no time to figure out the effect on individual programs and the students." Using averages, rather than real calculations based on concrete data, often works against the arts program. Always use accurate, actual figures when developing your proposals to determine the real effect of administrative proposals on the arts program.

Benchmark: A description that provides information for measuring the student's progress toward an established standard.

Block Scheduling: Block scheduling is one of several alternative ways to structure a student's time. It may take many forms, and the most common is the 4 x 4 system, or four courses per semester (up to eight courses per year). Each course in such a system is considered equivalent to a (former) full-year course. In another common alternative, block scheduling is referred to as the A/B system, in which students take up to eight courses per year, with classes meeting on alternative days for the entire year.

Bond Referendum: Election held to raise taxes for building construction or other capital expenses. (See **Levy Referendum.**)

Capital Outlay Fund: Accounts used for and/or restricted to additions or improvements of equipment, buildings, and sites. Portions of this budget are often allocated at the discretion of the local school principal. Many schools use capital outlay funds to purchase musical instruments and supplies; cuts in this fund can severely affect (or even eliminate) student music participation.

Categorical Aid: Restricted funds provided to school districts for specific purposes such as transportation, special education, vocational training, and others.

Central Administration: The administrator(s) and associated responsibilities for governance at the district level. This includes the superintendent and other directors with district-wide responsibilities.

Charter Schools: This reform movement advocates for the development of special schools that emphasize a specific curricular focus or learning environment. Local tax base support may be diverted to these charter schools, which may lead to long-term negative effects on public school budgets and to potential cuts (or even elimination) of music programs.

Class Size: The actual number of students in each teacher's classroom. Use of general fund monies is left to the discretion of the local principal. Depending on class size, he or she may decide to make further unpublished (or hidden) cuts in arts, particularly if averages are used rather than actual numbers.

Cocurricular: Curricular activities or events that occur outside the school day, but are not extracurricular. For example, public concerts, drama productions, and art shows are a natural outcome of curricular participation in music, theater, and art classes. They are an outgrowth of the arts curriculum and therefore should be considered part of the regular teacher's salary. Think of cocurricular activities as the equivalent of a final exam for a music performance class. (See **curricular** and **extracurricular.**)

Column: See **line item.**

Community Services Fund: Comprised of accounts that offer school district residents both recreational and educational community activities.

Core Requirements: Math, English, and science are the three subjects required and defined by federal, state, and sometimes even regional laws. Proficiencies in these three subject areas are tested on a regular basis and funding (or cuts) may be directly affected by a district's ranking. Under federal policy, music is considered a part of the core curriculum since the 1990s.

Criterion: A description of the standard of performance for a particular task.

Criterion-Referenced: Determining the value of a student's performance by referring to a requirement that was specified prior to the student's performance of a task.

Curricular: Normally refers to budget categories related to educational programs that occur during the regular class day. Curricular activities contribute substantially to the social, academic, intellectual, expressive, and communicative development of students. Music education is curricular. It is very important to maintain performance rehearsal time within the regular class schedule, since placing music activities outside the regular schedule leaves them open to redefinition as extracurricular and therefore more vulnerable to budget cuts. Examples of curricular music activities include classroom general music, music theory and history, music appreciation, and rehearsals of music organizations in preparation for cocurricular concerts (including the content and process of learning about the music). (See **cocurricular** and **extracurricular**.)

Debt Service Fund: Comprised of accounts related to retiring the bonds that are sold to construct the school buildings.

District-wide: A term used to describe any policy or decision that affects the entire district. For example, reductions in the district-wide budget may affect all arts line items in the entire district's budget, even those that may not specifically identify the arts.

Electives: Any curricular option that is not a required component of the curriculum.

Enrollment Decline: A reduction in the number of students enrolled in a district. Enrollment decline is often used as one justification for budget cuts. Budget cuts to the music program on the basis of enrollment decline are not justifiable—unless the loss of participation actually occurs within the music program itself.

Evaluation: The collection and use of information to make informed educational decisions.

Extracurricular: Activities held outside the regular school day in which public service or public relations is a primary purpose—even though, from the students' perspective, they may be a direct outcome of curricular activity. These activities may include any activity for which a "lump sum" stipend is made. Extracurricular activities are often confused or interchanged with cocurricular activities, but remember that their primary value is to create or nurture goodwill in the community. Each district needs to determine which activities of each organization fit into the cocurricular or extracurricular categories. (See **curricular** and **cocurricular**.)

"Feeder" Programs: Refers most commonly to programs for students in earlier grades that are designed to prepare them for higher-level participation in a particular area of study. For example, students enrolled in elementary band would then "feed into" middle school or high school band programs. The elimination of such feeder programs has a detrimental effect on further music participation in the higher grades.

Food Service Fund: Comprised of accounts related to the preparation and serving of school lunches.

Formative Assessment: Ongoing assessment within an educational program for the purpose of improving the program as it progresses.

Foundation Aid: Funds paid by the state to school districts and permitted to be used for operating expenses. The structure of this fund varies from state to state and changes frequently.

Frill: Do *not* use this term as it implies tacit agreement with a philosophy that is dismissive of, and damaging to, the value of the arts in a well-rounded educational system. Administrators may use this term as a way of illustrating that the arts are not part of the "basics," that is, reading, writing, and arithmetic. Using this term devalues the importance of the arts in students' lives.

Full-Time Equivalent (FTE): FTE is a measurement used to establish the financial value of teachers as a means of developing aspects of the budget related to personnel. Since FTE applies to both positions and programs, its importance cannot be overemphasized during the budget development process.

Fund Balance: The excess of the assets of a fund over its liabilities and reserves. (See **unappropriated fund balance** and **appropriated fund balance**.)

General Fund: Normally the largest source of revenues in the school district. These monies may be used to fund any needs within the school district, including salaries of education personnel and school district operations that do not have to be accounted for in another fund. Shortages in this fund most often lead to cuts in educational programs. The general fund includes nearly every budgetary category that affects the music program; it is therefore the most important budgetary category to understand and monitor.

Hidden Cuts: Refers to unspecified cuts that are (or may be) made in a music program and are not detailed in a published list of cuts. These decisions may be site-based and/or centralized, and are usually made after the board has adopted the final (district-wide) budget cut package. Key phrases to watch for are "increase class sizes," "changes in staffing ratio," and "reduction of teaching positions." If the local administrator (principal) chooses to make the entire cut in the music curriculum, he or she has the authority to do so once the staffing ratio is determined by the school board or central administration. A classic example of a hidden cut would be a line item such as this: "cut 3.0 FTE teaching positions" without specifying which teachers or programs would be reduced or eliminated.

Levy Referendum: An election held to raise taxes for the general operating fund. (See **bond referendum**.)

Line Item: Any single category included as a separate entry in the budget. (See **hidden cuts** for explanation of potential negative impact on music programming.)

Magnet Schools: This reform movement created specialized schools to emphasize a particular area, such as foreign language, mathematics, or science. Music is often eliminated from these schools, particularly if music making is philosophically perceived as only appropriate for the elite or for "gifted" students. On the other hand, districts that establish magnet schools for the arts often do so as a means of eliminating those programs for the general student population. This, in essence, may be interpreted as a breach of equal access regulations.

Measurement: The use of systematic methodology to observe musical behaviors in order to represent the magnitude of performance capability, task completion, and concept attainment.

Middle School Movement: This reform movement normally consists of a shifting of grades to place students from grades 5–8 or 6–8 in the same building unit. While it is often accompanied by some changes in educational philosophy, it is usually done to move children from overcrowded buildings into buildings that have space. Negative factors for music often include the elimination of elementary instrumental "feeder" systems, the elimination of the option for full-year participation in making music, and an explosion of exploratory mini-courses that reduce elective options for music students.

Music Administrator/Coordinator/Director: May include curriculum development, music coordinator, or other administrative positions, including department heads.

Norm: The midpoint in a set of scores taken from a large number of representative individuals where 50 percent of the scores are above the point and 50 percent are below.

Norm-Referenced: The value of a student's performance determined by referring to a norm established from a large number of representative individuals; this value indicates how a student performed in relation to other individuals' previous performances.

Participation Fees: See **"pay to play."**

"Pay-to-Play": One of the ways that school districts develop additional sources of revenue is to add participatory fees for cocurricular or extracurricular activities. While a philosophical case for "pay-to-play" may be made with extracurricular music activities, these fees cannot be financially or philosophically justified for participation in curricular or cocurricular aspects of the music program. Costs for those activities are, and should be, funded by the regular budget that provides teachers' salaries, usually the general fund. (See **curricular, cocurricular,** and **extracurricular.**)

Performance Assessment: An assessment that determines a student's ability to perform assigned tasks rather than his or her ability to answer questions.

Performance Task: A student demonstration that shows ability to handle complex material in real-world situations.

Portfolio Assessment: An analysis of a collection of student work used to demonstrate student achievement in a content area; student progress is determined by reviewing the collected works in light of previously established criteria.

Program Assessment: The determination of an educational program's strengths and weaknesses through a well-conceived and well-implemented plan of data collection and analysis.

Pupil-Staff Ratio (PSR): The school board establishes district-wide ratios to determine staffing needs based on the number of pupils in the district. The PSR is determined by the administration and approved by the school board. This ratio is normally the number of students per each 1.0 FTE position, including all staff as defined by the district. For example, if kindergarten students only attend school for one-half of each day, each student is the equivalent of .5 PU. It is used to calculate staffing needs based on the number of full-time students (or 1.0 pupil unit [PU] per student). The PU is the student figure used in the SFR and PSR. (See **full-time equivalent [FTE], student-faculty ratio [SFR],** and **pupil-staff ratio [PSR]**).

Ratio Point: The central administration establishes a student-teacher ratio for each school in the district based on financial values that relate to FTE (full-time equivalent) value, SFR (student-faculty ratio) and PSR (pupil-staffing ratio). These calculations identify the amount of funding equivalent to 1.0 FTE position, usually according to the dollar amount of the average teacher salary. The ratio point is the dollar value or cost of changing the ratio by one student. For example, a SFR of

28:1 means that the site will receive funding for 1.0 FTE position for each 28 students in the school. If the district increased the ratio to 29:1, the amount of money saved from that reduced funding is the cost of one ratio point. The district should have a figure available that indicates the financial value equivalent to any change in the ratio. This may be expressed as the financial value of 1.0 ratio point. (See **full-time equivalent [FTE]**, **student-faculty ratio [SFR]**, and **pupil-staff ratio [PSR]**.)

Reform Movements: Historically, there have been several different approaches to student scheduling, curriculum, and financing of schools; many of these have been shown to have a negative impact on the music curriculum. The most common reform movements are block scheduling, site-based management, middle schools, alternative scheduling, tax vouchers, charter schools, school-to-work programs, after school programs, and magnet schools.

Reliability: The consistency of an assessment instrument to obtain similar scores across time.

Rubric: A set of scoring criteria used to determine the value of a student's performance on assigned tasks; the criteria are written so students are able to learn what must be done to improve their performances in the future.

School to Work: This reform movement suggests that all or certain students should be forced to make career decisions (as early as grade 8) that would place them in a learning or vocational track for the remainder of their public education. In this reform model, music is not normally one of the school-to-work curricular areas— it is relegated to a special track reserved for "talented" students.

Secretarial/Clerical Staff: May include any designated aide, office or clerical workers and assistants, office supervisors, and so forth.

Self-Assessment: Analysis of one's own performance or abilities.

Site Administration: The administrator(s) and their associated responsibilities for governance at the local school level.

Site-Based Management: This reform movement trend moves more decision-making powers—including financial management—to the local school. The site administrator (or principal) bases his or her decisions on input from committees, which usually involve teachers and community members. It is crucial that committee membership represents the music program needs.

Standard: The content, level, or type of performance expected of students at a particular point in time or stage of development.

Standards-Based Assessment: Assessment established from school, district, state, or national standards of content and performance in a subject.

Student Assessment: The determination of one or more students' capabilities in a subject, made from information gathered on meaningful performance tasks that are referenced to well-defined, educationally sound performance criteria.

State Aid: Any grant made by a state government to another governmental unit.

Student-Faculty Ratio (SFR): This is the average number of students for each teacher. It is determined by dividing the number of pupil units (PU) by the number of teachers. Some districts may include nonteaching staff, such as guidance counselors, in the ratio.

Summative Assessment: Assessment performed to determine the overall effectiveness of an educational program.

Summer School: May include any summer arts program, including beginning instrumental music lessons. It may also include the addition of fees for participation. (See "**pay-to-play.**")

Transportation Fund: Comprised of accounts related to the pupil transportation program. If these monies are reduced or eliminated, it can negatively affect school marching or pep band programs, musical performances at away games, field trips, participation in state, regional, or national music competitions, and so on.

Unappropriated Fund Balance: Cash reserves not designated to any specific area of the budget. (See **appropriated fund balance** and **fund balance**.)

Unemployment Fund: Comprised of accounts related to unemployment compensation benefits for staff, teachers, and administrators who are unable to work (usually for health reasons) for a designated time period.

Validity: The effectiveness of an assessment instrument in measuring what it is supposed to measure; also relates to the appropriate use of assessment information and results.

Selected Resources

RESOURCES ON MUSIC ADVOCACY

Arts Education Partnership publications. www.aep-arts.org/Publications.htm.

Benham, John L. "The Advocates Plan." PowerPoint presentation with speech notes. In *Music Education Advocate's Toolkit: Strengthening Music in Your Community*. www .amc-music.org/advocacy/toolkit.htm.

———. *School Music and Reverse Economics*. Video, MENC, 1991.

Building Support for Music Education: A Practical Guide. www.supportmusic.com/ involved/index.html.

Education Commission of the States. http://ecs.org/ecsmain.asp?page=/html/ projectsPartners/chair2005/Huckabee.asp.

Keep Music Education Strong [pdf brochure]. www.supportmusic.com/ SM_Brochure.pdf.

Music Education Advocate's Toolkit: Strengthening Music in Your Community. www .amc-music.org/advocacy/toolkit.htm.

MENC: The National Association for Music Education website. www.menc.org.

SupportMusic.com, a public service of the Music Education Coalition. www.support music.com.

RESOURCES ON ASSESSMENT

Asmus, Edward. "Music Assessment Concepts." *Music Educators Journal* 86 (September 1999): 19–24.

Attachment E, Item 9. *ASCD Board of Directors Minutes*. March, 1989.

Barrett, Janet R. "Developing the Professional Judgment of Pre-service Music Teachers: Grading as a Case in Point." *Journal of Music Teacher Education* 15 (Spring 2006): 8–20.

Benham, S. J. "Musical Assessment as an Impetus for Strategic, Intentional, and Sustainable Growth in the Instrumental Classroom." In *The Practice of Assessment in Music Education: Frameworks, Models, and Designs*, edited by T. Brophy. Chicago: GIA Publications (in press).

Boyle, J. David, and Rudolf E. Radocy. *Measurement and Evaluation of Musical Experiences*. New York: Schirmer Books, 1986.

Colwell, R. "Assessment's Potential in Music Education." In *The New Handbook of Research on Music Teaching and Learning*, edited by R. Colwell and C. Richardson, 1128–58. New York: Oxford University Press, 2002.

———. "Music Assessment in an Increasingly Politicized, Accountability-Driven Educational Environment." In *Assessment in Music Education: Integrating Curriculum, Theory, and Practice*, edited by T. Brophy, 3–16. Chicago: GIA Publications, 2008.

Culver, Robert. *Master Teacher Profile*. Video. Available at www.reallygoodmusic.com/rgm.jsp?page=cdsvideosdetail&iid=123665.

———. "What Makes a Strong Program." Based on 1990 Sabbatical Research Report. Ann Arbor, MI: University of Michigan (Self-published).

Elliott, David. *Music Matters*. New York: Oxford University Press, 1997.

Froseth, James O., and Michael T. Hopkins. *Visual Diagnostics Skills Program—Brass*. Chicago: GIA Publications, 2004.

———. *Visual Diagnostics Skills Program—Woodwind*. Chicago: GIA Publications, 2004.

Goolsby, Thomas W. "Assessment in Instrumental Music." *Music Educators Journal* 86 (September 1999): 31–35, 50.

Gordon, E. E. "All about Audiation and Music Aptitudes." *Music Educators Journal* 86 (1999): 41–44.

———. *Music Aptitude and Related Tests: An Introduction*. Chicago: GIA Publications, 2001.

———. "The Nature and Description of Audiation." In *The Practice of Assessment in Music Education: Frameworks, Models, and Designs*, edited by T. Brophy. Chicago: GIA Publications (in press).

LeCroy, H. "Assessment and Strategic Planning." *Music Educators Journal* 86 (1999): 36–40.

Lehman, Paul R. "Issues of Assessment." In *Perspectives on Implementation: Arts Education Standards for America's Students*, edited by Bruce O. Boston. Reston, VA: MENC, 1994.

Lyman, Howard. *Test Scores and What They Mean*. Englewood Cliffs, NJ: Prentice Hall, 1991.

Walvoord, B. E. *Assessment Clear and Simple: A Practical Guide for Institutions, Departments, and General Education*. San Francisco: Jossey-Bass, 2004.

RESOURCES ON MUSIC RESEARCH

Altenmüller, E., and W. Gruhn. *Music, the Brain, and Music Learning*. GIML Monograph 2. Chicago: GIA Music, 2000.

Aron, A., and E. N. Aron. *Statistics for the Behavioral and Social Sciences: A Brief Course*. Upper Saddle River, NJ: Prentice-Hall, 1997.

Arts Education Partnership. *No Subject Left Behind: A Guide to Arts Education Opportunities in the 2001 NCLB Act.* www.aep-arts.org/files/advocacy/NoSubjectLeftBehind2005.pdf.

Consortium of National Arts Education Associations. *National Standards for Arts Education.* Reston, VA: MENC, 1994.

Elpus, K. "Improving Music Education." *Arts Education Policy Review* 108, no. 3 (2007): 13–18.

Gardner, H. *The Disciplined Mind: Beyond Facts and Standardized Tests, the K–12 Education That Every Child Deserves.* New York: Penguin, 2000.

———. *Intelligence Reframed: Multiple Intelligences for the 21st Century.* New York: Basic Books, 2000.

———. *Multiple Intelligences: New Horizons.* New York: Perseus Books, 2006.

Gee, C. B. "The 'Use and Abuse' of Arts Advocacy and Its Consequences for Music Education." In *The New Handbook of Research on Music Teaching and Learning,* edited by R. Colwell and C. P. Richardson, 941–61. New York: Oxford University Press, 2002.

Gordon, E. E. *Preparatory Audiation, Audition, and Music Learning Theory.* Chicago: GIA Music, 2001.

Jensen, E. *Music with the Brain in Mind.* San Diego, CA: Brain Store, 2000.

———. *Teaching with the Brain in Mind.* Alexandria, VA: Association for Curriculum and Supervision Development, 2001.

Levitin, Daniel J. *This Is Your Brain on Music.* New York: Penguin Group, 2007.

Mark, M. L. "A History of Music Education Advocacy." *Music Educators Journal* 89, no. 1 (2002): 44–48.

Mark, M. L., and C. L. Gary. *A History of American Music Education.* 3rd ed. Lanham, MD: MENC / Rowman and Littlefield Education, 2007.

Pinker, S. *How the Mind Works.* New York: W. W. Norton & Company, 1997.

Reimer, B. "The Danger of Music Education Advocacy. *International Journal of Music Education* 23, no. 2 (2005): 139–42.

Trehub, S. "Music on the Mind." *Newsweek,* July 24, 2000, 50ff.

Trehub, S., and Mary Hager. "Your Child's Brain." *Newsweek,* February 19, 1996, 54–61.

Wilson, Frank R. *Tone Deaf and All Thumbs.* New York: Penguin Group, 1986.

Index

About the Author

John Benham is generally recognized as one of the leading consultant advocates in saving school music programs. He received his bachelor of music with a double major in vocal and instrumental music education from Northwestern College (Minnesota), and his master of arts and doctor of education degrees from the University of Northern Colorado.

His diverse background includes nearly forty years of teaching experience. He has taught both the private and public sectors, taught both vocal and instrumental music in grades 5–12, and has served as a full-time and adjunct music educator at the university level. His related experience includes the fields of music retail, music instrument repair, and the manufacture of conducting batons.

He has presented at state, regional, and national conferences throughout North America, and has served on the national advocacy committees for both the American Choral Directors' Association and the American String Teachers' Association and is a member of the MENC Taskforce on Advocacy.

He is president and founder of Music in World Cultures, Inc., through which his global efforts in music education include consulting and teaching throughout the world.

Six years of service as a member of the board of directors of a metropolitan school district have provided him with valuable and practical insights into the inner workings of the public school system that have led to his successes as an advocate for saving music programs. His personal knowledge and experience provide unique understanding to help you go before a school board and administration with language they understand and methods that work.

Since beginning his efforts in 1981, he has provided consultant assistance in nearly every state and province in North America. He has worked with over 400 school districts in which his methods are responsible for saving over $70 million in budgetary reductions in music programs. As a result, over 2,000 music teachers and 500,000 students continue to make music each year. His successes in saving school music programs have been documented in the *Music Educators Journal, Music, Inc.*, the *Wind Instrument Retailer*, and *The Instrumentalist*.

He was awarded the Distinguished Service Award by the Minnesota Music Educators Association in 1994, and the Music Educators National Conference (MENC) in 1998. In 2003 MENC named him a Lowell Mason Fellow for his efforts in music advocacy. In 2010 the American String Teachers Association presented him with their National Advocacy Award.

In the words of the superintendent of schools with whom he served as a school board member, "As you learn the concept of reverse economics you will come to understand, as I do, that money is not saved by cutting music programs" (Burton M. Nygren, Superintendent of Schools, in *The Instrumentalist*, August [1991]: 18).

DATE DUE

Breinigsville, PA USA
16 November 2010
249411BV00002B/1/P